BrightRED Study Guide

CfE HIGHER

PHYSICAL EDUCATION

Jill Anderson and Rachael Ewing-Day

BrightRED
PUBLISHING

First published in 2016 by:
Bright Red Publishing Ltd
1 Torphichen Street
Edinburgh
EH3 8HX

A CIP record for this book is available from the British Library

ISBN 978-1-906736-76-7

With thanks to:
PDQ Digital Media Solutions Ltd (layout) and Project One Publishing Solutions (edit)

Cover design and series book design by Caleb Rutherford – e i d e t i c

Acknowledgements
Every effort has been made to seek all copyright holders. If any have been overlooked, then Bright Red Publishing will be delighted to make the necessary arrangements.

Permission has been sought from all relevant copyright holders and Bright Red Publishing are grateful for the use of the following:
Diagrams on pages 4, 9, 57, 65, 67, 68, 69, 70, 72, 74, 75, 93, 94 and 95 by ELEM design; Sonar512/iStock.com (p 6); Marianne Bevis (CC BY-ND 2.0)[1] (p 6); Cliff (CC BY 2.0)[2] (p 7); dgareri/iStock.com (p 8); graf/iStock.com (p 10); Serhiy Divin/iStock.com (p 12); AnikaSalsera/iStock.com (p 12); strickke/iStock.com (p 12); EarnestTse/iStock.com (p 13); Laszlo Szirtesi/iStock.com (p 13); joggiebotma/iStock.com (p 14); Brian McEntire/iStock.com (p 14); .shock/iStock.com (p 14); Republic of Korea (CC BY-SA 2.0)[3] (p 16); IPGGutenbergUKLtd/iStock.com (p 16); Berkut_34/iStock.com (p 17); Paisley Scotland (CC BY 2.0)[2] (p 18); AlexKalina/iStock.com (p 18); BaldBoris (CC BY 2.0)[2] (p 19); cokacoka/iStock.com (p 20); william87/iStock.com (p 20); Katherine Riley (CC BY 2.0)[2] (p 20); Aurelien Guichard (CC BY-SA 2.0)[3] (p 22); Jonathan Cardy (CC BY-SA 3.0)[4] (p 23); Poleydee (CC BY 4.0)[5] (p 24); Pierre-Yves Beaudouin (CC BY-SA 4.0)[6] (p 24); Robbie Dale (CC BY-SA 2.0)[3] (p 24); Paul Wilkinson (CC BY 2.0)[2] (p 25); Wildcow/iStock.com (p 25); SDAM/iStock.com (p 25); abezikus/iStock.com (p 25); IPGGutenbergUKLtd/iStock.com (p 25); barsik/iStock.com (p 26); StockPhotoAstur/iStock.com (p 26); saintho/iStock.com (p 27); PhotoBobil (CC BY 2.0)[2] (p 28); Tobias4242 (CC BY-SA 2.0)[3] (p 28); gertfrik/iStock.com (p 28); Clément Bucco-Lechat (CC BY-SA 3.0)[4] (p 29); AdamKR (CC BY-SA 2.0)[3] (p 29); Mihajlo Maricic/iStock.com (p 30); Ayakovlev/iStock.com (p 30); RuslanDashinsky/iStock.com (p 31); Bryan Pollard/iStock.com (p 32); AJ Guel (CC BY 2.0)[2] (p 32); gertfrik/iStock.com (p 32); Laszlo Szirtesi/iStock.com (p 33); dennisvdw/iStock.com (p 34); tankist276/iStock.com (p 34); Carine06 (CC BY-SA 2.0)[3] (p 34); AllegressePhotography/iStock.com (p 35); Marie-Lan Nguyen (CC-BY 3.0)[7] (p 35); Lena (CC BY-SA 2.0)[3] (p 35); Roman Stetsyk/iStock.com (p 35); jeancliclac/iStock.com (p 36); Christopher Lofthouse (p 37); Jeroen Bennink (CC BY 2.0)[2] (p 38); pointnshoot (CC BY 2.0)[2] (p 38); Snap2Art_RF/iStock.com (p 39); Rachael Ewing-Day (p 40); Berkut_34/iStock.com (p 41); Christopher Johnson (CC BY-SA 2.0)[3] (p 41); fourthandfifteen (CC BY 2.0)[2] (p 42); santirf/iStock.com (p 43); Craig Boyd (CC BY-SA 2.0)[3] (p 44); John Pavelka (CC BY 2.0)[2] (p 44); bradfordst219 (CC BY 2.0)[2] (p 45); Conor Lawless (CC BY 2.0)[2] (p 46); AndresRuffo/iStock.com (p 46); clsgraphics/iStock.com (p 48); Images on pages 48, 62, 72, 76 and 82 licenced by Ingram Image (p 48); almonfoto/iStock.com (p 50); Ronnie Macdonald (CC BY 2.0)[2] (p 52); CfE Higher Physical Education Course Specification © Scottish Qualifications Authority (p 52); los_bandito_anthony (CC BY 2.0)[2] (p 53); Carine06 (CC BY-SA 2.0)[3] (p 53); Jim Thurston (CC BY-SA 2.0)[3] (p 53); Groundhopper2000 (CC BY-SA 4.0)[6] (p 53); Jasmin Awad/iStock.com (p 54); Royal New Zealand Navy (CC BY-ND 2.0)[1] (p 54); istolethetv (CC BY 2.0)[2] (p 55); alexey_boldin/iStock.com (p 57); Andreyuu/iStock.com (p 58); Outdoor League/Cup Match Report Form © Scottish Hockey Union Limited (p 58); IR_Stone/iStock.com (p 60); NiroDesign/iStock.com (p 61); stevekingsman/iStock.com (p 62); Laszlo Szirtesi/iStock.com (p 63); Jon Candy (CC BY-SA 2.0)[3] (p 64); takasuu/iStock.com (p 65); kzenon/iStock.com (p 68); almonfoto/iStock.com (p 68); LuckyBusiness/iStock.com (p 68); wdeon/iStock.com (p 69); Two photos by AdamKR (CC BY-SA 2.0)[3] (p 69); johnthescone (CC BY 2.0)[2] (p 69); Brian McEntire/iStock.com (p 70); David W. Leindecker/Shutterstock.com (p 72); A.prestsaeter (CC BY-SA 4.0)[6] (p 76); OSTILL/iStock.com (p 78); Simanovskiy/iStock.com (p 79); K.M. Klemencic (CC BY 2.0)[2] (p 79); Michael Krinke/iStock.com (p 80); roibu/iStock.com (p 81); Matthew Wilkinson (CC BY 2.0)[2] (p 81); mangojuicy/iStock.com (p 83); Giakas/iStock.com (p 83); Brian Minkoff London Pixels (CC BY-SA 4.0)[6] (p 83); Austin Osuide (CC BY 2.0)[2] (p 83); Jason Clogg (CC BY-SA 2.0)[3] (p 83); lumaxart (CC BY-SA 2.0)[3] (p 86); mindscanner/iStock.com (p 86); Michael Cardus (CC BY 2.0)[2] (p 87); The Keep Calm-o-Matic (p 87); eenevski/iStock.com (p 88); Violka08/iStock.com (p 90); Chesky_W/iStock.com (p 90); muuraa/iStock.com (p 90).

[1] (CC BY-ND 2.0) http://creativecommons.org/licenses/by-nd/2.0/
[2] (CC BY 2.0) http://creativecommons.org/licenses/by/2.0/
[3] (CC BY-SA 2.0) https://creativecommons.org/licenses/by-sa/2.0/
[4] (CC BY-SA 3.0) http://creativecommons.org/licenses/by-sa/3.0/
[5] (CC BY 4.0) http://creativecommons.org/licenses/by/4.0/
[6] (CC BY-SA 4.0) https://creativecommons.org/licenses/by-sa/4.0/
[7] (CC-BY 3.0) http://creativecommons.org/licenses/by/3.0/

Printed and bound in the UK by Charlesworth Press.

CONTENTS LIST

INTRODUCTION

INTRODUCING CFE HIGHER PHYSICAL EDUCATION

DON'T FORGET

Key words from our curriculum are highlighted to assist you to see what is fundamentally important when delivering, completing or assessing the course.

AIMS AND STRUCTURE OF COURSE

The **main aims** of the CfE Higher Physical Education course are to enable you to:

- **develop** a broad and comprehensive range of complex movement and performance skills, and demonstrate them safely and effectively across a range of challenging contexts
- **select** and **apply skills** and make informed decisions to effectively perform in physical activities
- **analyse** mental, emotional, social and physical factors that impact on your performance
- **understand** how skills, techniques and strategies combine to produce an effective performance
- **analyse** and **evaluate** your performance to enhance personal effectiveness.

The course has two mandatory units and a course assessment. The mandatory units are:

- **Performance Skills**
- **Factors Impacting on Performance**

As the main purpose is to enable you to **develop**, **demonstrate** and **evaluate** performance, you will be assessed on how you **evaluate** and **analyse** when developing and applying strategies, techniques and skills to enhance your physical performance.

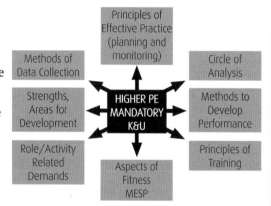

ONLINE

Visit www.brightredbooks.net to see Outcomes 1 and 2 in detail.

ONLINE

Head to www.brightredbooks.net to see the marks breakdown for the performance assessment.

FACTORS IMPACTING ON PERFORMANCE

The Factors Impacting on Performance paper assesses your ability to integrate and apply knowledge and understanding from across the course. It is designed to assess applied knowledge, understanding and evaluation skills. You will be required to demonstrate a range of approaches for developing or refining skills, fitness and performance composition strategies or tactics. You will be asked to analyse factors that have impacted on your performance and to analyse and evaluate factors that have impacted on performance whilst developing personal performance.

Students need to know about each of the **four factors** (mental, emotional, social and physical) that impact on performance, as each will be included within the assessment.

The question paper has two sections:

Section 1 Three questions, likely to be made up of two parts, which assess acquired and applied knowledge and understanding in solving performance issues.

Section 2 One question based on a scenario, which is likely to be related to the performance development process.

The paper accounts for 40% of the overall assessment.

To gain the award of the Course, you must pass both units as well as the course assessment. You are assessed on your planning and preparation, single performance and evaluating your performance before you will sit your exam.

PERFORMANCE SKILLS

The Performance Skills unit accounts for 60% of the overall mark and consists of three sections:

- Planning and preparation
- Single performance
- Evaluation

Planning and preparation

For the Planning and preparation section, you must be able to explain the relevance of two challenges you will face in your single performance and explain how you will prepare to meet these challenges. This will be completed in your school or college before you take part in your single performance and will be worth 8% of your overall grade.

QUESTION	ASSESSMENT ITEM	MARKS
1(a)	Explain the relevance of two challenges you will face in this single performance.	4
1(b)	Explain how you will prepare to meet these challenges.	4
	Total	8

Single performance

In the Single performance section, you must demonstrate **complex movement** and **performance skills**, related to your chosen physical activity. You must show you understand and can respond to the different nature and demands presented by the single performance and follow the rules, regulations and etiquette that apply to your chosen physical activity. The single performance has to be long enough to allow you to demonstrate the required skills. This will be whatever the norm is for your chosen physical activity. The context of the single performance must be challenging, competitive and/or demanding.

The table shows the outcomes and standards needed to meet to pass this section.

OUTCOME	ASSESSMENT ITEM	MARKS
2(a)	Demonstrate a broad and comprehensive performance repertoire (including complex movement and performance skills) during the performance.	8
2(b)	Demonstrate control and fluency of complex movement and performance skills during the performance.	8
2(c)	Demonstrate decision-making and problem solving throughout the performance.	8
2(d)	Demonstrate the effectiveness of following through on the decision-making during performance.	8
2(e)	Demonstrate the following of rules and regulations and displaying of etiquette during the performance.	4
2(f)	Demonstrate control of emotions during the performance.	4
	Total	40

Evaluation

The Evaluation element of the assessment requires you to carry out an evaluation in relation to the challenges you identified in the **planning and preparation** stage. This will be completed as soon as possible after your single performance and will be worth 12% of your overall grade. This need not be carried out immediately after the performance depending on particular circumstances.

QUESTION	ASSESSMENT ITEM	MARKS
3(a)	Analyse the effectiveness of your preparation for the two challenges explained in 1(a).	6
3(b)	Evaluate at least one strength of, and at least one area for development from, your performance.	6
	Total	12

DON'T FORGET

The purpose of the performance part of Course assessment is to assess your ability to plan, prepare for, perform and evaluate your own personal performance in one physical activity.

DON'T FORGET

What you write should not exceed one page of A4. This section is open book, so you will have access to your notes and resources when completing the task.

DON'T FORGET

Planning and preparing for performance is worth 8% of your overall grade.

DON'T FORGET

Evaluating your performance is worth 12% of your overall grade. There is no time restriction for completing this task, but markers advise that one page of A4 would be sufficient.

DON'T FORGET

Assessment for this unit consists of an external exam lasting 1 hour 30 minutes.

MENTAL FACTORS

MOTIVATION

INTRODUCTION

Mental factors in sport are what help sportspeople to be in the right frame of mind to perform. Mental factors can have a positive or a negative impact on a performance. **Mental fitness** is a state of mind in which we are open to **enjoying our environment** and the people in it, having the capacity to be **creative** and **imaginative** and to use our mental abilities to the fullest extent.

In this section we will look at these sub-factors:

- motivation
- decision-making and information processing
- concentration and focus of attention.

DON'T FORGET

You may have concentrated on other mental sub-factors throughout your course. Make sure you know the factor that is most relevant to your activity and personal performance needs.

Andy Murray competed in six Grand Slam finals before he finally won the Wimbledon Championships in 2013. Ask yourself what might have happened to Andy Murray if he had lost his motivation to continue to chase his dream.

MOTIVATION

In order to succeed in sport, you need to want to perform and to improve your performance. The determination to do this is called **motivation**. Motivation can be defined as a combination of the drive within us to achieve our aims and the outside factors which affect it. Motivation is made up of:

- **extrinsic** (external) motivation, such as money, prizes, acclaim, status, praise
- **intrinsic** (internal) motivation comes from within, such as the determination of an athlete driven by the want to be the best. Financial rewards would not be a contributing factor for this athlete.

An athlete driven by both forms of motivation can achieve their goals. However, the athlete who is driven purely by external factors may struggle when the circumstances become more demanding as they will find it difficult, if not impossible, to find the determination to work through the challenges.

Positive impacts on performance

Possessing a high level of motivation will ensure that you continually work hard until you succeed, as you have the drive to achieve your goals. You will continually get up early, stay up late, and travel for miles in order to train. A unique drive within you will ensure that you persevere when training gets difficult and you face lots of setbacks, such as injury, losing streaks or poor weather and resources. Being motivated has a positive impact on your performance as you maintain resilience and a drive to train hard and push yourself out of your comfort zone. This push is what is required of elite athletes and it ensures you continue to progress and rise to new challenges.

contd

"I have missed more than 9,000 shots in my career. I have lost almost 300 games. On 26 occasions I have been entrusted to take the game winning shot, and I missed. I have failed over and over and over again in my life. And that is why I succeed."
Michael Jordan

ONLINE

Follow the link at www.brightredbooks.net to read more about Michael Jordan's quote.

ONLINE

Visit www.brightredbooks. net to see a model answer regarding motivation from a team game.

DON'T FORGET

To remain self-motivated you need to be positive. This will help you to be in the right mindset. You must also be confident. This will give you the belief that you can achieve your goals. You must also 'be hungry'. You need to want to do it and to go out and get it!

ONLINE TEST

Test yourself on your knowledge of mental factors that impact on performance at www.brightredbooks.net

Negative impacts on performance

Having a lack of motivation or being motivated purely by external factors can have a negative impact on performance when things do not go the way you expect. You may not put in the required effort in order to improve, and blame external factors, time, money or facilities for this. The only way you will develop and improve your performance is to train, but when you lack motivation you may not train properly, and as a result you will be badly prepared for competition. This will result in you eventually being beaten in competition and losing further motivation.

Placing a value on a task can also have an impact on a person's motivation. If the task is not valued, the motivation for the task will probably be low.

THINGS TO DO AND THINK ABOUT

Using the model example below, generate examples for how motivation could have a positive and negative effect on your performance in an individual activity of your choice.

Positive impact on performance	Negative impact on performance
Having a high level of motivation helped my performance within my team. Being highly motivated, even in difficult and challenging situations, enabled me to support my team mates by continuing to work to my best ability. Even when we were losing the match, I refused to give up and I continued to look for fast break opportunities as well as sprinting back up court to carry out my role in zone defence. This increased our chances of getting back into the match. Also when I became tired in the later stages of the match, having a high level of motivation helped me to ignore any negative thoughts in my head and maintain a high level of performance for a longer period of time.	Having a low level of motivation had a negative effect on my performance within my team. I find it difficult to play to the best of my ability especially under demanding circumstances such as when losing the match or becoming fatigued. We were playing man to man defence and my opponent was much faster than me. This meant that they could take the ball and run past me easily to create scoring opportunities. I became demotivated as I couldn't stop them. This led to me putting little effort into trying to mark my opponent as I knew they would get passed me anyway. As a result, my team became frustrated with me as they were left to cover my man. We ended up falling out and team morale was at a low. We had no chance of getting back into this match.

DECISION-MAKING AND INFORMATION PROCESSING

DECISION-MAKING

Decision-making can be defined as an action or process of choosing a preferred option or course of action from a set of alternatives. It forms the basis of all deliberate and voluntary behaviour. Good quality decision-making is a critical skill in any sport. The quality of your decisions has a huge impact on your results. Experience plays a significant part in the decision-making process, and sometimes you need to make the wrong decision before you learn when to make the right one. This means that when you are in the same situation again, you will be able to make the appropriate decision more quickly.

Positive impacts on performance

When decision-making has a positive effect on your performance, you will carry out the correct action for the given situation. You will observe and assess the situation before deciding on the best course of action to take. For example, in a badminton match, you will watch the position of your opponent and play the shuttle away from them. You will put them under pressure to return a shot which could lead to you winning a point.

Developing experience in making decisions and solving problems helps you become quicker at making them, and depending on your sport, there may be many situations where speed of thought has a major impact. Even when you are placed in challenging situations you will remain calm, take in all cues and logically decide on how to cope. Selecting the right decision for any given situation is more likely to lead to success. For example, in football or basketball, passing to an unmarked player rather than a marked player reduces the chances of losing possession. If you make the right decision on a regular basis you will retain possession of the ball, maintain control of rallies, and generally succeed at outwitting your opponent.

Negative impacts on performance

Making poor decisions can often lead to the loss of possession or loss of points, baskets or goals. In team games, a poor decision made when passing out from defence can lead to an interception and a 1 vs 1 situation on your goal. If you choose a technique that is slow to execute then you may give your opponent more time to recover and prepare themselves to respond to your action. This negatively impacts on your performance as your objective is to deny time and space to opponents.

When decision-making affects your performance in a negative way, you will struggle to decide the best action you should take. This can lead to a 'hit-and-hope' situation where your actions become involuntary. For example, in netball when you have a tall defender in front of you, you might just throw the ball high somewhere to get rid of it within three seconds. Panic sets into your performance and your ability to think quickly and logically is severely hampered. You will fail to put your opposition under any pressure and will most likely lose the match.

INFORMATION PROCESSING

Information processing is used to consider how learning and development takes place, and is closely linked to many other mental factors. The information processing model described below links together four parts as a learning loop:

- **input** – the brain processes information (gathered through the senses) and lists possible options
- **decision-making** – a decision is made to carry out the best possible option and the muscles initiate a response
- **outcome** – the action is completed and the performer sees the result
- **feedback** – if correct, the action is repeated. If wrong, the action is changed.

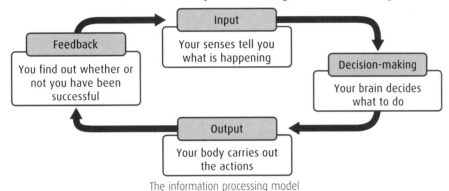

The information processing model

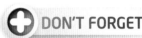

Decision-making is subconscious when you are at the automatic stage of learning.

Positive impacts on performance

When your information processing is automatic, your attention will be freed so that you can concentrate on the tactical elements of your game. This will make you less anxious about performing skills or techniques in certain situations. You will be calmer and mentally better prepared to meet the demands of the competitive situation.

 ONLINE TEST

Test yourself on your knowledge of mental factors that impact on performance at www.brightredbooks.net

Negative impacts on performance

If your information processing is slow your performance will also be slow. You will over-think certain decisions and will lose the advantage over your opponent if you are unable to respond quickly. This will affect your ability to fulfil your role and individual responsibilities effectively, which may result in you or your team losing valuable points.

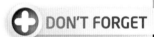

Think of your brain acting like a computer. What information do you need to put in for you to get from A to B? Place yourself on a court or a pitch in your chosen activity and think of the real situations that you are faced with to help you answer this.

Volleyball

	Positive Impact on Performance	Negative Impact on Performance
Input	I watched the opposition, taking in as many cues as I could. I looked at the position of the setter and also which hitter was likely to hit the spike. I also watched the height and direction of the ball.	I watched my back court team mate play the ball to my setter. I was looking at my setter to see if they were going to set the ball to me. I also watched to see if the opposition were setting up a block.
Decision making	I recognised the setter was playing a back set to the hitter on the right side of the court. As the setter I decided I should step across to my team mate to set a double block on the right side of the net.	I decided that I was going to spike the ball and I began to think about my positioning.
Output	Carrying out of the decision. I stepped across to the right and jumped alongside my teammate to set the double block	I moved back off of the net while watching the flight of the ball. I then began my run up and jump towards the ball.
Feedback	The block was successful. We both jumped at the optimum time i.e. we were at the top of our jump as the hitter played the ball. This meant that our hands were well above the net blocking the area and cutting down the space for the hitter to play the ball to. As a result, the ball deflected off of our hands and landed on the opponent's court and we scored a point.	My spike was unsuccessful. I jumped too early and I was on the way back down before I contacted the ball. This meant that my spike went into the net and we lost the point. Next time I need to time my run up to leave a split second later so that I am at the top of my jump when I contact the ball.

THINGS TO DO AND THINK ABOUT

Using the volleyball example above, generate examples to demonstrate how information processing could have a positive and negative effect on your performance in an activity of your choice.

CONCENTRATION AND FOCUS

OVERVIEW

Concentration can be defined as the ability to stay on task. Being able to completely focus your attention on something for a period of time. When athletes concentrate fully they can take in all the information they need to make good decisions, such as responding to their opponent or adapting to their environment. It is the ability to pay particular attention to the task in hand.

Concentrating on the right things at the right time is one of the most important skills an athlete can possess. All athletes recognise that they may have difficulties concentrating for the duration of a performance or at specific times. Difficulties in concentrating are usually due to distractions. Rather than concentrating on appropriate cues, athletes may become distracted by thoughts, emotions and other events. These distractions can be both internal and external.

INTERNAL DISTRACTIONS	EXTERNAL DISTRCTIONS
Living in the past – worrying about old mistakes	Visual – crowd, competitors, scoreboard etc
Living in the future – focussing on results or outcomes	Auditory – talking, laughing, traffic, phones etc
Self-talk – inner monologue that is negative	Gamesmanship – rude comments, jesting etc
Arousal levels or anxiety – narrows attention field so you miss environmental cues	
Fatigue – focussing on physical effort detracts from tactical considerations	

ACTIVITY

1   Imagine you are about to represent your country in an activity of your choice. You are about to compete for the gold medal. What thoughts might go through your head? List the positive and negative thoughts.

2   Think of a time when you competed under pressure, such as in a particular sports performance, or in your single performance. What thoughts are going through your head? List the positive and negative thoughts.

Different sports require different types of concentration:

- **Sustained concentration** - distance running, cycling, tennis, and squash.

- **Short bursts of concentration** - cricket, golf, shooting, athletic field events.

- **Intense concentration** - sprinting events, bobsleigh and skiing.

Positive impacts on performance

When an athlete has the ability to concentrate, they are able to focus completely on the performance and can ignore any distractions that are going on around them. Their skill level will remain high and they will make good decisions throughout the performance due

VIDEO LINK

Why do these sports require sustained concentration? See if you can understand why Andy Murray needed sustained concentration to win the rally. Watch the clip at www.brightredbooks.net

VIDEO LINK

Watch the clip at www.brightredbooks.net that highlights why golfers' concentration levels are required in short bursts.

VIDEO LINK

Watch the clip at www.brightredbooks.net and imagine what could happen if these skiers did not possess intense concentration levels.

contd

to their ability to remain on task and think about what they doing. They will be able to use their past experiences of particular situations and then select and apply the best skills and techniques to be performed. Their minds will remain clear as they will be calm and they will have a positive mindset.

Negative effect on performance

Losing concentration within a performance will result in an athlete performing below their ability. They may forget what they should be doing or they may execute skills poorly by not focusing on the job at hand. If they do not concentrate on their opponent they will make poor decisions when trying to beat them. This will also lead to a drop in confidence when things start to go wrong and the performer feels that they have lost the match. Frustration will set in when a performer knows that they are underperforming.

 THINGS TO DO AND THINK ABOUT

1   Generate examples to demonstrate how concentration and focus could have a positive and negative effect on your performance in an activity of your choice.

2   Select a mental factor to describe and explain. Write an answer that relates to an activity of your choosing. Answers must include the following information:
    ● a definition of the sub-factor
    ● an explanation of how it can positively impact on your performance
    ● an explanation of how it could negatively impact on your performance.

3   Read through your answer and try to expand further on the positive and negative impacts. Provide another example from the same activity to demonstrate how this factor can impact positively or negatively.

4   Compare your answer to this model answer:

> **Badminton – Positive effect on performance**
> I am an experienced player and during the game I am able to observe my opponents movements and based on their actions and weaknesses select the most appropriate shot to play, even in demanding situations/contexts. This good decision making makes it more likely I will be able to move my opponent around the court by playing the shuttle into space. This would limit their ability to select and execute the most appropriate shot as they may be moved out of position. This therefore increases my chances of winning the rally and ultimately the match.
>
> **Badminton – Negative effect on performance**
> I often make wrong decisions when I am under pressure. I just return the shuttle rather than thinking what shot would be best to play. This often results in me playing the shuttle high to the centre of my opponent's court which sets them up to play attacking shots against me. This puts me under more pressure and panic begins to affect my performance further. As a result, this severely hampers my chances of winning individual rallies and ultimately the match as a whole.

Think about the following things:
● Have you applied the factor to your chosen activity and also explained the impact on your performance?
● Are your descriptions as detailed?
● Do you relate the factor to your role within the activity of your choosing?

5   Repeat Questions 2, 3 and 4 with another factor.

6   Explain these two factors and how they impact on your performance to a family member or friend. Try not to look at your notes and encourage them to ask questions.

 **DON'T FORGET**
Concentration levels will vary depending on the pressures that the athlete feels. These can be internal or external.

 ONLINE TEST
Test yourself on your knowledge of mental factors that impact on performance at www.brightredbooks.net

 ONLINE
Visit www.brightredbooks.net to read more information on mental toughness and anxiety and its impact on performance.

 **DON'T FORGET**
A drop in concentration will negatively affect other mental factors. You should include this in your answer.

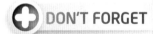 **DON'T FORGET**
In preparation for the exam you should know about at least two mental sub-factors in depth.

 ONLINE
Head to www.brightredbooks.net for more examples of model answers.

EMOTIONAL FACTORS

HAPPINESS, SADNESS AND ANGER

When performing there are a number of emotional factors that can impact on your performance. How you feel inside can directly affect your ability to execute your skills automatically and deal with the demands of your performance. In any activity, your emotional state plays a crucial part in determining your success. This section will explain a few emotional sub-factors:

- happiness and sadness
- anger
- fear
- trust

DON'T FORGET

You may have studied other sub-factors which also fall into the emotional factor category.

VIDEO LINK

Watch the video clip at www.brightredbooks.net that highlights some emotions being demonstrated before, during or after sporting performances.

VIDEO LINK

Check out the clip showing sadness in an individual activity, where the margin between happiness and sadness is sometimes very small at www.brightredbooks.net

VIDEO LINK

Watch the clip at www.brightredbooks.net showing great moments in football, both happy and sad. Ask yourself what is the difference between these emotions.

HAPPINESS AND SADNESS

In all competitive activities where there has to be both a winner and a loser, you may experience immense happiness or sadness as a result of your performance. Happiness or sadness can be defined as an emotional state of mind that ranges from feeling content and joyful to feeling despair or sorrow. Both emotions can be character building and can help you to develop the motivation to train harder in order to reach your potential.

Positive impacts on performance

Happiness will affect your performance positively as it can impact on emotional factors such as your confidence, self-belief, resilience, levels of optimism, and your ability to realise your potential. For example, being in a happy state of mind before performing will increase your confidence in your own ability to execute your skills successfully, under the pressure of a crowd, and the demands of the competition. Happiness has the benefit of making you very optimistic and when you are in this frame of mind you are more likely to continue on this winning streak.

Negative impacts on performance

The opposite of happiness is sadness. This is most likely to have a negative impact on your performance, because it can negatively affect your confidence, self-belief, resilience, concentration and ensure that you are pessimistic about your chances of success. When you are sad you are caught up in a negative emotion which can affect your ability to concentrate and focus on the job at hand. For example, if you are still sad about a previous poor performance during a gymnastics competition, then you will be less able to refocus and concentrate on the next piece of apparatus in order to complete the competition, and perform to your best. Low confidence can affect your self-belief in your ability to perform your skills successfully, resulting in a poorer level of skill execution. This will ensure you receive fewer points from the judges and will lead to you and being defeated by your competitors.

ANGER

Anger is a strong emotion that can affect your performance both positively and negatively. It can be defined as a feeling of annoyance, displeasure or hostility. This uncomfortable emotion is often demonstrated after being provoked. An individual may have been offended, denied, wronged and as a result they can react in retaliation. Anger can be seen in many different ways during performance. It could be a player shouting at themselves or opponent, physically lashing out, or even increasing the power in their next skill, when this exertion is not required.

contd

Positive impacts on performance

Anger in sport can be a very useful emotion when used in the right way. In order for it to positively affect your performance, players must channel their anger into motivation. Players who can control their anger will be much more effective, as they can retain the upper hand over their opponents. During a match, players will psych themselves and each other up at key moments in the game, in order to get one another angry. They may visualise other things, or remember certain events in order to bring on this anger. They do this, so that together they are encouraged and determined to exert their maximum force, without holding anything back. It results in them running their opponents back, gaining possession and having a psychological advantage over their opponents. This advantage can result in winning more points, baskets or goals and winning the fixture.

Negative impacts on performance

Anger without control and restraint will negatively affect performance, as it damages decision-making capabilities. Opponents will look for ways to irritate you in order to put you off your game plan, affect your skill execution or your concentration. This is a common tactic, sometimes called 'psyching your opponent out'. Players have to be aware of this and be clever about the way they react if they are annoyed by other players, or by decision from officials, and other external factors that are out with their control.

During team games, a strong player may be regularly targeted to be man-marked and ultimately wound up during the contest. This can lead to this player getting frustrated by being constantly professionally fouled. If this player retaliates and lashes out, the only winner is their opponent, as they have done their job of getting the strongest player sent off from the game. Their team will then be at a major disadvantage as they will be a very strong player down and more likely to concede goals, baskets or points.

THINGS TO DO AND THINK ABOUT

1   Complete the table to connect some words that make you happy or sad. The first example has been completed for you.

Sad	In order to achieve this, I/we will be	Happy
Losing	Training regularly	Winning
		Playing well
Getting injured		
	Working as a team	

2   In your chosen activity, explain what makes you happy and how this positively impacts on your performance.

3   In your chosen activity, explain what makes you sad and why this negatively impacts on your performance.

4   Explain to a classmate, friend or family member what is meant by anger in sport.

5   Look at the list of behaviours below, categorise them into positive examples of anger or negative examples of anger. Think of as many as you can:
   - taking deep breaths
   - calming your aggression
   - fouling your opponent
   - shouting at official
   - being strong and assertive
   - fighting with opponents or teammates.

6   Describe what happens when anger positively impacts on your performance.

7   Describe what happens when anger negatively impacts on your performance.

DON'T FORGET
Happiness will make you optimistic about success; sadness may make you more pessimistic.

DON'T FORGET
Anger can be demonstrated in many different ways.

VIDEO LINK
Watch the clip at www.brightredbooks.net that shows athletes being aggressive during performance. Decide whether the example is either positive anger or negative anger.

DON'T FORGET
Successful performers will find ways of channelling this anger into their performance.

DON'T FORGET
Smart performers control their anger and let their performance do the talking.

ONLINE
Read the information on anger during sporting performance at www.brightredbooks.net. What tips are suggested?

VIDEO LINK
Watch the clip at www.brightredbooks.net showing table tennis players getting angry.

ONLINE TEST
Test yourself on the emotional factors impacting performance at www.brightredbooks.net

FEAR AND TRUST

FEAR

Fear is an unpleasant emotion caused by the threat of danger, pain or harm. In sporting terms it can be induced by a perceived threat, which can cause you to operate a 'fight-or-flight' coping mechanism. The threat perceived could be of being physical hurt, emotionally scared, socially embarrassed or mentally weakened. Fear has the ability to positively and negatively impact on your performance. When it works for you it can produce endorphins that will assist your ability to concentrate on your performance, or it can hinder you by limiting your ability to focus on the task of performing.

Learning to cope with fear is essential for successful performers, as risk-taking is a fundamental component of being creative and ultimately successful. Being scared and wary of performing are natural emotions. However, the level of nerves can also indicate the level of endorphins and adrenalin that will be running through your body.

Positive impacts on performance

This positive energy, excitement and ability to relish all challenges, can impact on a performer's focus and ability to peak at the correct time. When athletes can manage this fear and turn it into an opportunity, then they will try new skills, experience more success and gain increased confidence and self-belief. By taking positive risks, the athlete is empowered to influence the contest and perform to their best.

VIDEO LINK

Watch the clip at www.brightredbooks.net showing a 7-year-old girl overcoming her fear to complete her very first ski jump. What does she do and tell herself repeatedly in order to complete the jump?

For a gymnast to win, they must perform their skills in new and creative ways, so that they stand out from their competitors. However, this means that in training they need to try new and challenging skills regularly which will undoubtedly be scary and at times painful. Nevertheless, when it comes to the competition they are emotionally prepared as they have experienced and overcome their fear. They will be confident and prepared to meet the demands of the competition and score the maximum points they are capable of.

DON'T FORGET

Being fearful is natural. You can train yourself to view scary situations as challenges that need to be faced.

Negative impacts on performance

Fear can produce negative thoughts which can impact on your mentality and ability to meet your performance demands. Winning and losing is so important in most competitive settings that fear of failure or fear of not performing well is at the forefront of an athlete's mind. The thought of making mistakes in front of teammates, coaches and spectators can be so paralysing that the player sits inside their comfort zone just doing the bare minimum. Fear of failure prevents performers from pushing themselves onto the next level. Their performance becomes reactive to their opponent. This allows the opposition to take control and dictate the direction of play so they have the upper hand, resulting in them eventually winning the competition.

DON'T FORGET

Fear will negatively impact on your performance when it hinders you from trying new and creative things.

TRUST

Trust is essential for successful performance or training in all activities. It can be defined as the reliance on the integrity, strength, surety or confidence in another person or thing. So for teams to perform successfully together they must trust in one another's ability, and for individuals to perform they need to trust in their equipment, coaches and apparatus.

Positive impacts on performance

Trust between team members is vital. When team players value the unique talents and contributions of each team member, then the team will work more cohesively as a unit, resulting in a higher level of performance and wins. As players trust each other and are sure of one another they will begin to read each others' actions more accurately and react to support their team-mates before their opponents can react. For example, a volleyball player may look to set their opponents up to try for spikes at the net, because they know and trust that they have excellent spikers in these positions. They are confident in their spikers' ability to rise and hit the spike, securing the point for the team and win the game.

Negative impacts on performance

Without trust between team-mates performances will lack cohesion and synchronicity. This can mean that opponents find gaps in your defensive structures which they can exploit to score baskets, points or goals. Losing too many of these will result in the teams losing their games.

In football the goalkeeper is generally responsible for coming out to collect crosses within their reach. When their defenders do not trust in their ability to do this without making a mistake, they may decide to try to do the goalkeeper's job for them. In this instance, both players will try to clear the same ball, which could result in neither of them doing it successfully and their opponents gaining possession in a dangerous area, where scoring is likely.

 DON'T FORGET

Having trust will positively impact on your performance, whilst not having trust will negatively impact on your performance.

 THINGS TO DO AND THINK ABOUT

1   Recall and list a variety of situations that may occur that you may be fearful in. For example attempting a new and dangerous skill for the first time.

2   Suggest things that you could do to ensure this situation was less scary.

3   Think about your role within your chosen activity. Explain how fear can:
    (a) positively impact on your performance
    (b) negatively impact on your performance.

4   Provide examples from your chosen activity that explains how having trust positively impacted on your performance.

5   Provide examples from your chosen activity that explains how not having trust negatively impacted on your performance.

 ONLINE TEST

Complete the Sports Emotions Questionnaire at www.brightredbooks.net

ONLINE

Visit www.brightredbooks.net to read further about surprise another emotional factor that impacts on performance.

SOCIAL FACTORS

CO-OPERATION, ROLES AND RESPONSIBILITIES

DON'T FORGET

You may have studied other sub-factors which also fall into the emotional factor category.

VIDEO LINK

There are many social benefits to participating in sporting activities. Watch the clip at www.brightredbooks.net to outline a number of them.

DON'T FORGET

Social factors can be split into the interactions with others and the traditions within sports.

INTRODUCTION

Socially there are many factors that impact on our performance which can affect us both positively and negatively. Our interactions with others, the traditions of the sport, officials, spectators and our coaches all play a part in our performance.

Social factors that impact on performance can be separated into two categories:
- those which deal with your social interactions with others
- those which relate to the traditions of activities within society.

By understanding how those around us can influence our choices and actions you will be better prepared to develop the social factors that impact on your own performance. This chapter will deal with some of the social factors that could influence your performance. These factors are shown in the table.

INTERACTIONS WITH OTHERS	TRADITIONS IN SOCIETY
Co-operation	Roles and responsibilities
Inclusion	Etiquette
Leadership	

CO-OPERATION

Co-operation is necessary for successful participation in many games and physical activities. This can be defined as the ability to work together with others towards a joint purpose or goal. Co-operation is essential in team activities, as it enables teams to effectively execute the team tactics and strategies. Teams that display excellent co-operation skills include players who trust one another to fulfil their individual roles. This means that, as a whole, the team will successfully perform the tactic or strategy they have adopted.

Positive impacts on performance

Co-operating can also be used when learning new skills. During racket sports, players often help each other by feeding the ball so they can practice their shots. The main aim is to help make learning easier for a partner or team-mate so they can practice the skill without any pressure. If every player in a team is supported and encouraged to develop and improve, the team as a whole will co-operate more effectively with one another and perform with success.

Additionally, teams that can co-operate socially by encouraging, motivating, supporting and praising each member's effort equally will unite against their opponents. This will

contd

ensure that everyone is valued and determined to do their best, to the benefit of the whole team. If all players understand that they can influence how their team-mates feel and encourage, instead of criticising and getting angry, then all players will perform to the best of their ability. When this happens a team can remain positive and be confident in their own ability to succeed and win.

Negative impacts on performance

When playing the strategy of zone defence within a team game, each player is responsible for protecting their own zone within the defensive area. If a team member is unable to co-operate, then they would fail to communicate with team-mates to let them know when opponents move into their zone. This lack of cohesion would negatively impact on the team's ability to work together and move as a unit. The result being that gaps would arise in their defensive area that their opponents could exploit.

ROLES AND RESPONSIBILITIES

Within teams and activities it is essential that individuals perform their unique role consistently well. Roles and responsibilities can be defined as the ability to perform your individual job within your team. Roles can be playing or non-playing as there are many people who can contribute to successful performance. We will focus on playing roles and the responsibilities which could be held by your position or your social role as a captain or vice-captain.

Positive impacts on performance

A team's ability to perform their individual roles and responsibilities effectively can have a positive impact on the performance. In team invasive games, your defenders must ensure they mark the opposing players and prevent them from scoring goals (or baskets or points). Your defenders, midfielders or forwards all have a unique job to do in order to deny space to your opponent. The success of the team will be due to all playing roles being performed successfully, resulting in you creating more chances to score more goals (or baskets or points) than your opponents and successfully winning the game.

Negative impacts on performance

The failure to perform your individual roles and responsibilities could also have a negative impact on your performance. For example, you may be given the responsibility for taking the free kicks (or penalty corners, penalties or free throws) because of your consistency in training and because you are the best person for this job. However, if the pressure of the occasion gets to you and you do not convert these chances your team will have missed valuable opportunities. If these opportunities do not present themselves again in the game then your team may lose or draw the fixture.

DON'T FORGET
Even within the same team, roles and responsibilities will vary.

DON'T FORGET
Think about activities from your course or your own experience that you are familiar with. You have to be able to explain what your roles and responsibilities are.

ONLINE TEST
Test yourself on your knowledge of social factors that impact on performance at www.brightredbooks.net

THINGS TO DO AND THINK ABOUT

Complete the table to help you think about how you co-operate and take responsibility for your own role within a range of activities. The first example has been completed for you.

ACTIVITY	ROLE	RESPONSIBILITY	HOW DID YOU CO-OPERATE?
Volleyball	Captain	Communicate the change in tactic during performance.	Listened to coaching team, responded to instructions, communicated to others.
Dance	Crew member		
	Player		Maintained a rally with my opponent so we could both warm up.
		Taking the free throws/kicks/penalties.	
		Creating and scoring goals/baskets/points.	
	Goalkeeper		

INCLUSION AND LEADERSHIP

INCLUSION

VIDEO LINK

Watch the clips of footballers and volleyball players celebrating scoring a goal/point at www.brightredbooks.net. Which sport is most inclusive?

When everyone in a team feels included and that their performance is valued, this will positively impact on the whole team's success. Inclusion can be defined as the act of including or being involved in a group or structure. Regardless of ability and experience, every performer should feel equally important and feel that they have a large contribution to make towards their individual and team goals. Inclusion in sport should occur regardless of race, gender, ethnicity, disability or ability. Everyone has a right to experience the mental, emotional, social and physical benefits that sport delivers. Inclusion may also mean that everyone is actively involved in the cycle of analysis that underpins any development plans. Inclusion is when every member is consulted in order to develop a shared vision regarding their individual and team targets and goals.

VIDEO LINK

Watch the inspirational clip at www.brightredbooks.net that highlights how some athletes participate against many odds. Ask yourself if you have achieved all you are capable of achieving in your chosen activity.

Positive impacts on performance

Having an inclusive team can positively impact on your performance as it values the contribution of all team members and makes players feel equally as important and included. For example, when teams include all members in the celebration of a point (or goal or basket), there will be high fives or pats on the back for each member equally. This team recognises that without every player holding their position and contributing to the build-up play, the scoring opportunity would never have presented itself in the first place. Teams that include everyone in the celebration for a point (or goal or basket) during the game ensure that all players have a sense of belonging by being involved in a social group. This positive reinforcement can motivate players to play to the best of their ability. If every player can do this, the combined effort of the group will result in a successful team performance.

Negative impacts on performance

When players feel like they are not included or part of the team, relationships and morale can be low because individuals may feel isolated and undervalued, and that they are unable to contribute to the team effectively. During competitive performance, a player's feelings can heavily impact on their performance and their ability to focus and concentrate on the job at hand, so the feelings of isolation can negatively influence their physical performance and they can underperform. When this happens, the underperforming player can feel even more isolated as they might be blamed for the team's poor performance and left out even more. These players can become disillusioned very quickly and it can result in them firstly not enjoying practice, then not showing up and eventually quitting the team or activity.

LEADERSHIP

Leadership is another social sub-factor that can impact on performance. Leadership can be defined as the act of guiding people towards an agreed team goal. The relationship between players and those with a leadership role, such as captains, coaches, managers or officials, can positively or negatively influence your performance. Leaders need to be positive role models who lead by example and therefore set high standards of effort, determination and resilience. When leaders are respected, players will follow them and the team will be united and able to work as a single unit.

Positive impacts on performance

A coach's leadership style can directly influence the morale and determination of an athlete, and the relationship with your coach can be instrumental to your success as a performer. When coaches are positive, encouraging and committed, whilst able to appropriately challenge the athlete, the athlete will strive to achieve their full potential. This is because this athlete feels like they are capable and supported. Coaches will strategically set small, measurable, achievable, realistic and time-phased targets that will prepare their athlete for competition. They will then instinctively know when to increase the challenge and move the performer on. This positively impacts on the athlete's performance as they continually strive to achieve a new and more difficult target and goal, thus avoiding a performance plateau. In short, they continually develop, improve and peak at the important competition phases of their season.

Negative impacts on performance

The leadership of a captain could negatively impact on the performance of a team. Their job is to be the link between the coaching team and the players, and to remain calm and in control at all time. When the captain displays a lack of emotional control then it can negatively influence the rest of the team as players will look up to and respect the captain. A captain must put the team goal before their own emotions and ensure they are guiding the team towards their performance goals. When the captain becomes a negative role model on the pitch, the team can start to fragment and follow this bad example. They may start focussing on small external factors outwith their control, such as a decision made by the official, and can feel like they are being victimised and penalised unfairly. The impact on the performance of the team is that they lose focus, concentration and fail to outwit their opponents, in order to win the game.

VIDEO LINK

Watch the clip of Kelly Brown a former captain of the Scotland rugby team speak about his role as captain at www.brightredbooks.net

DON'T FORGET

Refer to what happens to skills and player's mindsets when the competition becomes more heated.

THINGS TO DO AND THINK ABOUT

1 List a number of ways that you can include all team-mates in practice and performance.

2 Explain how this will positively impact on the whole team's performance.

3 Explain when this does not happen, how performance will be negatively impacted.

ONLINE TEST

Test yourself on your knowledge social factors that impact on performance at www.brightredbooks.net

ETIQUETTE AND RELATIONSHIPS

ETIQUETTE/ETHICS

Most sports have their own unwritten rules regarding the etiquette that is required from participants. Etiquette can be defined as the customary code of accepted behaviours followed in society by members of a particular group. These are usually traditions that ensure athletes follow an appropriate code of conduct and perform in a sporting and fair manner. Rugby teams traditionally form tunnels and clap their opponents off the pitch; in judo, opponents bow to one another. Generally, shaking hands with opponents and exchanging a few words is custom, whilst players can also be seen to clap and show appreciation to the crowd. Additionally, you can demonstrate good ethics (morals) during the game by accepting the decision of the official, treating all players, coaches and officials with respect, adhering to the written rules of the game, owning up to any mistakes or assisting your opponent when they are injured or have fallen.

Positive impacts on performance

VIDEO LINK

Head to www.brightredbooks.net and watch the clip of what a player does when awarded a free kick for something he does not agree with. Ask yourself what you would do in his position.

Adopting a positive and ethical approach to competition can ensure that you behave fairly and win in a sporting and decent manner. Sporting etiquette can positively impact on your performance because it ensures that the welfare and safety of all players remains more important than winning. During competition, if your opponent gets injured it is customary to place the ball out of play to allow the player to receive treatment and for the team to regroup. Technically, this is not in the official written rules of any games, but it is an internal value that could be applied to sporting contests. In response to this gesture of goodwill, the team that received treatment generally play the ball back to the opposition when play is resumed. It can positively impact on your performance because you have a quick period of time to reflect on the game so far and iron out anything which may not be going to plan. These periods of time can be invaluable to the success of your overall performance.

Negative impacts on performance

In pursuit of a victory, some athletes will resort to actions than are less than desirable in order to win. Performers are finding new and creative ways to cheat and gain an advantage over their opponents. Some examples include taking performance enhancing drugs, committing professional fouls, faking injuries, lip-reading team talks, spying on training, bribing officials and even poisoning their opponent's food! Not enough people are playing to the rules in mainstream activities and this means that it becomes too easy for opponents to forget their own integrity and join in. Nevertheless, when found out for these actions performers can be stripped of all their titles and this can leave their reputation tarnished. All the hard work and training they have participated in would have been for absolutely nothing.

RELATIONSHIPS

Relationships are the ways in which two or more people or groups regard and behave towards one other. A relationship can be defined as the way in which two or more people are connected. Socially, our relationships with one another can directly influence our ability to co-operate, communicate and work together during our performance.

Positive impacts on performance

Relationships can have a profound impact on the potential success of your performance. When players, coaches and the crowd are positive and encouraging to one another, then the performer is motivated to do their best and achieve their potential. In aesthetic activities like dance, ice-skating or gymnastics, there is a relationship between the performer and the music. The performer can use the tempo, rhythm and speed of the music as stimuli in their performance. This can increase the aesthetics of their dance and allow their feeling and emotions to be portrayed.

contd

Negative impacts on performance

In many individual activities, performers spend a lot of one-on-one time with their coach. If you do not get along or if you have different visions for the future, you question each other's comments and motives. When players do not completely understand the purpose of what they have been asked to do, they may not fully commit to training or the tactic. When coaches and players cannot be open and honest with each other, this will impact on their ability to work together to utilise the strengths of the player and to succeed. Similarly in aesthetic activities if there is a poor relationship between the music and the performer, the performer may be out of time, faster or slower than the tempo and may select moves that do not fit with the mood of the music. Can you imagine trying to ballet dance to Metallica?

THINGS TO DO AND THINK ABOUT

1 Complete the table. The first example has been completed for you.

ACTIVITY	ETIQUETTE (positive impact)	POOR CONDUCT (negative impact)
Football	Shaking hands at the end of the match.	Diving to fool the referee into awarding a free kick.
	Returning the ball/shuttle to opponent when it is their serve.	
		Stamping on your opponent during a scrum.
	Remaining quiet when your opponents perform.	
Swimming		
	Playing the ball out if you see someone is injured.	

2 Describe to a friend or family member what is meant by etiquette and how it can positively or negatively impact on your performance.

3 Complete the table to help you examine relationships. The first example has been completed for you.

RELATIONSHIP (role)	POSITIVE	NEGATIVE
Coach	Motivates you to succeed	Hinders your self-belief
Captain		
Parent or Carer		
Friend		
Team-mate		

4 Select a social factor to describe and explain. Write down an answer that relates to an activity of your choosing. Answers must include the following information:

   ● a definition of the sub-factor

   ● an explanation of how it can positively impact on your performance

   ● an explanation of how it could negatively impact on your performance.

5 Read through your answer and try to expand further on the positive and negative impacts. Provide another example from the same activity to demonstrate how this factor can impact positively or negatively.

6 Repeat Questions 2, 4 and 5 with another factor.

7 Explain these two factors and how they impact on your performance to a family member or friend. Try not to look at your notes and encourage them to ask questions.

PHYSICAL FACTORS

PHYSICAL FITNESS AND CARDIO-RESPIRATORY ENDURANCE (CRE)

DON'T FORGET

You may be familiar with other aspects of skill-related fitness. Use the information that is best suited to your role and activity.

ASPECT OF PHYSICAL FITNESS	ASPECT OF SKILL-RELATED FITNESS
Cardio-respiratory endurance	Co-ordination
Strength	Agility
Flexibility	Reaction time
Muscular endurance	Balance
Speed	Core stability
Power	

DON'T FORGET

Different activities and specific roles within these activities demand different aspect of fitness.

DON'T FORGET

Within your course you may have studied other sub factors that will also fall into the physical factor category.

VIDEO LINK

If you are interested in finding out more about how the heart and lungs work then you can watch the clip at www.brightredbooks.net

DON'T FORGET

Your body must have an efficient oxygen transport system for your CRE to be a positive aspect of your performance.

PHYSICAL FITNESS

When performing and competing against others, your fitness level is an essential component to your success. There are many different aspects of fitness and indeed factors within these different aspects. In every activity or sport, and in varying roles within these activities, a different aspect of fitness will be required, because the demands of activities vary and different strengths are essential.

In this section we will look at the Physical factor, which is a general state of health and wellbeing and the ability to perform aspects of sports or activities without undue fatigue. Physical factors can be split into two categories:

● those that relate to your aspects of physical fitness

● those which relate to your aspects of skill-related fitness.

In this section we will look at the sub-factors listed in the table, and explain how they can positively or negatively impact on your performance.

CARDIO-RESPIRATORY ENDURANCE (CRE)

Cardio-respiratory endurance (CRE) is the ability of the heart and lungs to provide the working muscles with oxygenated blood for a prolonged period of time. As you breathe oxygen into your lungs, the blood in your heart is oxygenated before it gets pumped around your body. You need this in activities that last a long time because it ensures that oxygen gets delivered to your muscles to help them keep going, while it also takes away lactic acid, the waste product, from these muscles. This supports your muscles to work continuously and ensure that lactic acid does not cause stiffness or cramps that could hinder the performance of your muscles. This process of delivering oxygen and taking away lactic acid is called the **oxygen transport system**. The energy required to fuel your body during this process is supplied **aerobically** (with oxygen).

Positive impacts on performance

High levels of CRE delay the onset of fatigue and ensures that your concentration, control, touch and decision-making remain positive. When your CRE is above average and in the very good and excellent categories of the national norms tables, you will be able to not only keep up with your opponent but surpass them and ensure they are aiming to keep up with you. Being able to maintain a consistent work rate throughout the competition will ensure you finish as hard as you started. This will result in you going on to win the competition or fixture.

contd

Negative impacts on performance

Poor CRE will result in the performer becoming breathless more quickly and unable to keep up with play or maintain a high skill level. It may also affect decision-making as the tiredness can impact on the ability to concentrate on tactical considerations. If you have below average CRE you may need longer rest periods before you are able to perform at your best. This will have a negative effect on your performance as you will be less able to keep up with your opponent and respond instinctively to their movements, resulting in them having more time and space to execute their own skills and exploit the space left in your playing area. This space and time will allow them to control the competition and create scoring opportunities that will ensure they win the fixture or race.

 ## THINGS TO DO AND THINK ABOUT

1 Look at the table below that explains why CRE is necessary in activities. Analyse the explanation and tick whether it is describing a positive or negative impact on performance and write down what activity is being described.

EXPLANATION OF THE IMPACT OF CRE ON PERFORMANCE	POSITIVE	NEGATIVE	ACTIVITY
I am unable to keep jogging around the pitch towards the end of the game therefore I walk and this means that my opponent is unmarked.			
I repeatedly work aerobically to maintain an effective stride pattern that is technically proficient and conserves my energy for my sprint finish.			
I fatigue towards the end of the game and this means that I make unforced errors and lose possession of the ball easily.			
I maintain a high skill level throughout my performance and consistently get back into the ready positions after every shot in order to prepare myself.			

2 Describe how CRE has an impact on your performance in an activity of your choice. In your answer, make sure you:

- provide a definition of CRE

- explain in detail how CRE positively impacts on your performance

- explain in detail how CRE can negatively impact on your performance.

3 Think like an exam marker. Look at the sample answers at www.brightredbooks.net. Rate the sample answers in order of which will achieve the best marks and which will receive the least marks.

 ### VIDEO LINK

Watch the video clip at www.brightredbooks.net that explains briefly what endurance and stamina is.

 ### VIDEO LINK

Watch the clip at www.brightredbooks.net showing an athlete suffering from insufficient CRE as she finishes the marathon. State a few things that happen to her body as a result of exhaustion.

 ### DON'T FORGET

Cardio-respiratory endurance is sometimes referred to as the abbreviated term CRE.

 ### ONLINE

Check your answers at www.brightredbooks.net

 ### ONLINE TEST

Head to www.brightredbooks.net to test your knowledge of the fitness factors which impact on performance.

FLEXIBILITY AND MUSCULAR ENDURANCE

FLEXIBILITY

Flexibility (also known as suppleness) can be defined as the range of movement across a joint, and refers to the pliability of joints to stretch and bend without breaking. Flexibility not only needs exceptional range of movement across joints, but it also needs muscles to be supple and stretchy to allow this mobility across joints. There are two types of flexibility:

- **Static** flexibility is necessary when you are holding a part of the body still. This predominately requires stretchy supple muscles to contract and hold the body position.
- **Dynamic** flexibility uses the full range of movement across a joint for a short time within an overall performance. This requires a combination of the stretchy, supple muscles and pliable joints that will not break.

POSITIVE IMPACTS ON PERFORMANCE

Static flexibility is required in aesthetic activities where you have to hold your body still during various balances. For example, a good range of movement is needed across the hips to be able to perform aesthetic balances. When the range of movement is excellent you will score more marks from the judges, resulting in you performing well in competitions.

Dynamic flexibility is required for those who play in a variety of directly competitive activities. Having a large range of movement across all joints will mean that performers can get themselves into unusual positions and shapes to perform skills with maximum power and strength, they will be able to perform the appropriate preparation, action and recovery required for success. This will positively impact on their performance as they can bend, twist and extend their limbs in order to perform with maximum power, strength and accuracy, so that they can perform their skills and techniques efficiently and deny their opponent time to react. This ultimately leads them to scoring more points (or goals, tries or baskets) and win the competition.

Negative impacts on performance

Poor flexibility can result in injuries when the muscles are overstretched. If this happens, you become unable to perform and if you are in a team then your team will need to perform without you. Furthermore if you are unable to extend, stretch or reach for the ball or shuttle then you will be less likely to return objects that are dispatched at you, just out with your reach. Your lack of flexibility will impact on your range of movement and your ability to perform the appropriate preparation, action and recovery to ensure accuracy and power in your skills. Your skill execution will be poor and you will fail to win points.

MUSCULAR ENDURANCE

Muscular endurance is the ability of a muscle or group of muscles to perform repeated contractions for extended periods of time without tiring. When your muscles work continuously for a long period of time they endure a lot of cramp and pain, which is a result of lactic acid build-up. Actions that you perform repeatedly that require muscular endurance include running, jumping, side-stepping, swimming, cycling, passing, punching, shooting, blocking, smashing and so on. Having muscular endurance means that muscles rid themselves of lactic acid quickly, enabling you to continue performing effectively for the duration of the performance.

Positive impacts on performance

In activities that require you to perform repeated actions, muscular endurance enables you to do this continually, whilst maintaining your speed or exertion level. This is because your muscles are efficient at ridding themselves of lactic acid, the

contd

VIDEO LINK

Watch the clip at www.brightredbooks.net that demonstrates dynamic and static flexibility and control.

DON'T FORGET

Two types of flexibility are static, used to remain still, and dynamic, used during movement.

waste by-product that can hinder performance. As your muscles and mind can withstand the pain that comes from the production of lactic acid, you will be able to repeat actions consistently well, so your performance will be the same at the end of your performance as it is at the start. This positively impacts on your performance as you maintain a high skill, stroke or stride level and secure valuable points, goals, basket or time, for yourself or your team during competition.

Negative impacts on performance

If muscular endurance is below average, the performer will be unable to make effective use of their muscles during their performance. For example, when swimmers, runners, cyclists and rowers have poor muscular endurance, they will be unable to exert the same effort into each stroke or stride, resulting in them needing to take more strokes or strides to complete the same distance. These additional strokes or strides would continue to fatigue them and they would be unable to finish the race as quickly as they started. The overall impact on their performance will be negative, as they fail to secure a fast time.

 THINGS TO DO AND THINK ABOUT

1   Look at the following images and tick the box that best categorises the type of flexibility being demonstrated. Explain why this is.

EXAMPLE	STATIC	DYNAMIC	EXAMPLE	STATIC	DYNAMIC

2   How does flexibility impact on your performance in an activity of your own choice? In your answer, make sure you:
    - provide a definition of flexibility
    - explain in detail how flexibility positively impacts on your performance
    - explain in detail how flexibility can negatively impact on your performance.

3   Explain your thinking to a friend, family member or teacher, justifying the correct order.

4   How does muscular endurance impact on your performance in an activity of your own choice? In your answer, make sure you:
    - provide a definition of muscular endurance
    - explain in detail how muscular endurance positively impacts on your performance
    - explain in detail how muscular endurance can negatively impact on your performance.

VIDEO LINK

Watch the clip at www.brightredbooks.net to see the British men's team demonstrating exceptional muscular endurance to win gold in the team pursuit at the 2012 Olympics.

DON'T FORGET

Actions that you perform repeatedly, such as running, swimming, cycling and rowing, require muscular endurance.

ONLINE

Think like an exam marker. Look at the sample answers at www.brightredbooks.net. Rate the sample answers in order of which will achieve the best marks and which will receive the least marks. You can check the answers once you are finished.

ONLINE TEST

Test your knowledge of the fitness factors which impact on performance at www.brightredbooks.net

STRENGTH

OVERVIEW

Strength is another main component of physical fitness. It can be defined as the maximum force a muscle or group of muscles can exert at any one time. It can be explained as the toughness and brawn of performers to withstand great force or pressure and maintain stability. Strength influences performance in many activities as it relates directly to the capacity of the muscles. When the muscles are strong they can withstand lots of physical exertion and can be relied upon to apply power and force.

Strength can also impact on your performance in activities where you push against a surface, object or person in order to apply force and project the object, surface or person away from you.

Strength can be further divided into:
- **static** strength (muscles contract and hold one position)
- **dynamic** strength (muscles repeatedly apply force over a short period of time)
- **explosive** strength or power (muscles exert force in a short, fast burst).

POSITIVE IMPACTS ON PERFORMANCE

When performers are strong they can withstand tackles from opponents and this will make them stronger on the ball and able to retain possession for long periods of time. In team games, strength can push your opponent back into their own half and can ensure that you win 50/50 balls and gain possession at crucial phases of the game. This possession will ensure that their team will be more successful at creating scoring opportunities that will enable them to win the game.

Strength in your muscles is a great way to prevent injury. When the muscles around your joints are strong they protect the joint from the trauma of repetitive action and twists and turns. This positively impacts on your performance as it enables you to keep training and developing for competitions, even when the pressure you are under is intensified.

NEGATIVE IMPACTS ON PERFORMANCE

Without strength a performer would be unable to hold a specific skill for the desired length of time. Performers of subjective activities (such as gymnastics) would not be able to perform static balances for the appropriate length of time because their muscles cannot contract and hold the weight of their body as they balance. This will result in them gaining fewer marks from the judges for the execution of this skill, which would in turn impact on their overall score for their performance and position in the competition.

A performer without strength would be more inclined to get injured, as their muscles would be unable to protect their joints from the impact of performance. This will negatively impact on your performance as you will be unable to keep training and developing your performance in order to play in games, and potentially missing out on important competitions.

 THINGS TO DO AND THINK ABOUT

1 Look at the table below that explains why strength is necessary in activities. Analyse the explanation and tick whether it is describing a positive or negative impact on performance. Then write down what activity is being described.

EXPLANATION OF THE IMPACT OF STRENGTH ON PERFORMANCE	POSITIVE	NEGATIVE	ACTIVITY
I use strength to assist me when defending. It ensures I remain strong and stable when tackling, this mean my opponent rarely scored against me.			
I work anaerobically to exert maximum force possible on my opponents. This ensures I push them deep back into their area and we have the advantage of a few more metres on them.			
I cannot hold my balance skills for a long period of time. This means I do not gain the maximum points available from the judges for this element.			
I am not able to shoot with much force or accuracy, because I lack strength in my muscles. The result is my shots are much easier for keepers to save.			

2 How does strength impact on your performance in an activity of your own choice? In your answer, make sure you:
  - provide a definition of strength
  - explain in detail how strength positively impacts on your performance
  - explain in detail how strength can negatively impact on your performance.

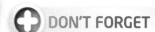 DON'T FORGET

You can demonstrate strength by withstanding powerful actions and out-muscling opponents. Strength in the muscles also helps to prevent injury.

 ONLINE

Check your answers at www.brightredbooks.net

 ONLINE TEST

Head to www.brightredbooks.net to test your knowledge of the fitness factors which impact on performance.

SPEED, SPEED ENDURANCE AND POWER

SPEED AND SPEED ENDURANCE

Speed can be described as the rate at which a body can perform an action over time. When performers can move or operate quickly they will deny their opponents time and will be able to execute skills and techniques more efficiently. Speed can be split into two categories:

- **whole body speed**, where your whole body performs an action quickly
- **limb speed**, when a particular part of your body performs an action quickly.

Speed endurance is the ability to sustain maximum speed or near maximum speed for a prolonged period of time. Performers who have excellent speed endurance will be able to continually make fast explosive sprints over a long period time. The energy required to do this is supplied **anaerobically** as the aerobic system is too slow to meet the energy demands. Repeated movements results in lactic acid build-up which leads to muscle fatigue. Speed endurance (anaerobic endurance) is the ability of the body to delay the production of lactic acid or to develop a tolerance to higher concentrations of it.

POSITIVE IMPACTS ON PERFORMANCE

Speed is required in team invasive games when trying to beat an opponent to a 50/50 ball. When your speed is very good you will lose a defender easily, get into space to support an attack, be able to dribble around an opponent and chase back to close down an attack. This will help your team to maintain possession and create scoring opportunities, resulting in you winning the fixture.

In directly competitive central net games speed will also assist you to get to the ball or shuttle as quickly as possible. This will allow you more time to concern yourself with your preparation, action and recovery and tactical considerations. Ultimately this will positively impact on your performance as you will make the most appropriate decisions and perform your skills consistently well.

In athletics, cycling and rowing speed endurance will be required to maintain a consistent stride or stroke pattern throughout the whole race. When your speed endurance is good your body will be efficient at getting rid of lactic acid from the muscles or will be able to block out the pain and continue performing and complete the race when you are in extreme pain.

NEGATIVE IMPACTS ON PERFORMANCE

When you lack speed you will be unable to perform an action in a short period of time. In racket sports when you attack the net you would be unable to respond to the ball or shuttle being returned to you quickly. This would result in you failing to manoeuvre and get into the appropriate position to execute the technique effectively, therefore losing the point.

In racing events if you lack speed in short distance races then you would fail to perform your actions quickly and travel quicker than your opponents. Your inability to move your muscles and limbs at speed would affect the preparation, action and recovery of your technique and you would not move as efficiently as other competitors. This will negatively impact on your performance as you will fail to win or place highly during the race.

POWER

Power can be defined as an action that is the result of a combination of speed and strength. It could also be described as the ability to travel or produce great speed or force. When you exert maximum muscular contraction instantly in actions such as jumping, striking, throwing, kicking or rotating, you demonstrate power. Power enables you to propel yourself or an object, in a desired direction and gain distance, height, speed and rotation. These gains are required to meet the demands of your performance in a wide variety of activities.

Positive impacts on performance

In throwing, striking or jumping activities, explosive force and dynamic speed at the point of take-off or release of an action will ensure your performance is positively impacted. Along with a speedy preparation, when you apply the greatest maximum force possible to your action, an equal and opposite reaction will occur and you will propel yourself or your object in the desired direction, resulting in a successful distance, height or quality of rotation being performed that can beat other competitors. In racket sports this single action will propel an object through the air and gain the furthest distance possible. This distance will ensure that you outperform your opponent or push them to the back of their court and into a defensive position where they are less likely to win the point.

Negative impacts on performance

Power can negatively impact on your performance as you may overhit your shots and continually hit them out of the back line of your opponents court, drive the ball past the green, or pass the ball too quickly for your team-mates. On these occasions the result will be that you fail to apply the appropriate weighting to accurately execute your skill and meet the performance demands.

Performers that do not have power may fail to meet the demands of their performance.

In aesthetic activities power is required to gain height off the ground in jumps and rotations as this scores higher marks from the judges. If you struggle to generate speed and strength in the preparation stage of your action, you will not produce the maximum force you are capable of. This could result in you not gaining enough height and therefore time in the air to rotate efficiently with straight limbs. This can result in you under rotating and not executing the landing of your skills, which in turn will affect your score negatively.

 DON'T FORGET

Any action that requires you to combine the two physical sub-factors strength and speed will involve power.

 VIDEO LINK

Watch the clip of Jessica Ennis demonstrating excellent power during her long jump performance at www.brightredbooks.net

DON'T FORGET

Power would be required for activities such as the shot putt, golf, javelin, hammer or smashes in racket sports, and it is also useful for providing an effective start in sprints.

 ONLINE TEST

Head to www.brightredbooks.net to test your knowledge of the fitness factors which impact on performance.

DON'T FORGET

When developing your **physical fitness** performance it is important that you understand the **phases of training** (pp 70–71) and the **principles of training** (pp 74–75).

 THINGS TO DO AND THINK ABOUT

1 How does speed impact on your performance in an activity of your own choice? In your answer, make sure you:
- provide a definition of speed or speed endurance
- explain in detail how speed positively impacts on your performance
- explain in detail how speed can negatively impact on your performance.

2 How does power impact on your performance in an activity of your own choice? In your answer, make sure you:
- provide a definition of power
- state the skill or technique you are going to refer to
- explain in detail how power positively impacts on your performance
- explain in detail how power can negatively impact on your performance.

SKILL-RELATED: CO-ORDINATION

SKILL-RELATED ASPECTS OF PHYSICAL PERFORMANCE

There are six skill-related fitness components:

- co-ordination
- reaction time
- timing
- agility
- balance
- rhythm

Skilled performers typically excel in all six areas. We will look at co-ordination, reaction time and agility in this section

CO-ORDINATION

Co-ordination is the ability to control your body whilst linking a series of movements or subroutines together. When you move your body parts in an appropriate order it will ensure that you successfully execute complex skills and perform them with consistency and fluency. Co-ordination most often involves body parts performing different actions at the same time in order to execute a particular action, skill or movement. For example, your arms maybe be following different rhythms, patterns or pathways than your legs and your brain will be co-ordinating all of this activity at exactly the same moment.

There are different types of co-ordination:

- **hand-eye** co-ordination is predominately required in striking, racket sports or activities using your hands to catch
- **foot-eye** co-ordination, used in activities where you kick
- **thigh-eye**, or **chest-eye** co-ordination, required in activities where you use extended parts of your body.

Positive impacts on performance

Co-ordination is particularly important when performing a complex skill or when performing a skill or action at speed. Performing the correct skill or technique in a variety of activities requires a great deal of coordination. In swimming, your arms must work to complete your stroke pattern whilst your legs work differently to produce the kicking movement. When these different actions are performed simultaneously, with control, fluency and at speed then your technique will be efficient and you will remain in a streamlined position as you cut through the water quickly. This technique will ensure that you gain as quick a time as possible and beat your competitors.

DON'T FORGET

All complex and serial skills that have multiple subroutines require co-ordination.

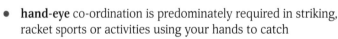

VIDEO LINK

Watch the clip at www.brightredbooks.net that shows a performer demonstrating fluency as they link movements together to maintain control of a football.

DON'T FORGET

You can have hand-eye, foot-eye or thigh/chest-eye co-ordination.

In directly competitive activities co-ordination ensures that you can link subroutines together and perform complex skills fluently, with control and rhythm. High levels of co-ordination ensure that you automatically perform complex skills and techniques and that you can free your attention to deal with tactical considerations. The ability to do this can positively impact on your performance.

Negative impacts on performance

Poor co-ordination can result in performers hesitating when it comes to performing certain skills or techniques. This hesitation can cost them as they fail to move with control, fluency and rhythm. This lack of control can give opponents an advantage over you as you may perform your skills with less power and accuracy. Lacking power or accuracy will result in your skills being less effective and you failing to retain possession of the ball or win the point. If this continues you or your team will fail to win the fixture as you have been unable to remain in control of your performance. In subjective activities, a lack of co-ordination results in you scoring fewer marks from the judge. Skills will not link together smoothly or look as aesthetically pleasing.

 THINGS TO DO AND THINK ABOUT

 ONLINE TEST

Head to www.brightredbooks.net to test your knowledge of the fitness factors which impact on performance.

1   Examine the list of activities below. With a partner discuss what type of co-ordination the different activities require, **hand-eye**, **foot-eye**, **chest-eye** or **thigh-eye**. Justify your answers and explain your thinking.

football	dancing	ice-skating	sprinting
hockey	cycling	rowing	basketball
volleyball	rugby	trampolining	

2   How does co-ordination impact on your performance in an activity of your own choice? In your answer, make sure you:

- provide a definition of co-ordination.

- state the skill or technique you are going to refer to

- explain in detail how co-ordination positively impacts on your performance

- explain in detail how co-ordination can negatively impact on your performance.

SKILL-RELATED: AGILITY AND REACTION TIME

AGILITY

Agility is the ability to change the position of the body quickly, precisely and with control. Agility uses a combination of speed, flexibility and strength to solve movement problems such as defenders, objects or apparatus. It affects your nimbleness and your ability to move at speed with grace. This can help performers dodge opponents, retain their balance and move dynamically, when they are responding to performance stimuli.

DON'T FORGET

Agility can also describe your mental capacity. When you have mental agility you will be able to think about numerous things at once and change your mind and decisions quickly.

Positive impacts on performance

Agility helps when competing in activities as it enables you to change direction quickly whilst maintaining balance and control. A player who is agile can also respond more quickly to an opposing player, close down an opponent, stop, change direction and explosively increase speed when required. It helps a performer move around their playing area smoothly and quickly in order to anticipate movement and reach for an object to save a point, goal or basket. When a performer can do this it will positively impact on their performance as they will consistently return shots and frustrate their opponent as they will assume that they have played a winner.

Negative impacts on performance

A lack of agility would make it difficult for a player to reach objects played into the corners of their playing area or that have been returned quicker than expected. If this was the case the player would fail to return shots and lose the point. This would mean that they are continually under pressure which will eventually result in them losing the game.

Goalkeepers in many activities require agility to quickly manoeuvre themselves around their goal. When agility is poor they will fail to get down low to block a shot and back up to enable them within a split second to react and save the rebound effort. This is because their mental and physical agility is not quick, efficient or graceful enough to meet the demands of their position. This would result in them being unable to save shots that test this agility and their team losing vital goals in games.

VIDEO LINK

Watch the clip at www.brightredbooks.net showing a performer completing an agility course and demonstrating control, speed, flexibility and strength as they find solutions to the problems posed by the obstacles.

ONLINE

Check out examples of the impact of agility on performance at www.brightredbooks.net

REACTION TIME

Reaction time can be defined as the time it takes for a performer to respond to a stimulus and then perform the movements selected. The stimulus is received through the performers sight, hearing or kinaesthetic awareness. Reaction time is positive when a performer pays attention to relevant cues and is able to control their anxiety. A performer's reaction time is also shorter when there is only one possible response and this response is well practiced, while it may be longer if there is more than one possible response and the performance situation is new and unfamiliar. Reaction time can be decisive between winning or losing in an activity.

contd

DON'T FORGET

Reaction time is required at the start of activities that require you to race against others and anytime during activities that are directly competitive.

Positive impacts on performance

A skilled performer has a quick reaction time by reacting to a stimulus, selecting a response and moving sharply. Goalkeepers in many activities need quick reactions in order to move at speed to prevent goals. Within a split second they have to judge where the ball is going, interpret and respond to the wind speed and trajectory of the ball, before reacting and moving in order to stop it from entering their goal.

An example of simple reaction time is at the start of races when the starting pistol goes off. Having a good reaction time will allow you to move as quickly as possible without false starting. This will give you an instant advantage over other competitors, particularly in short sprints, when every centimetre counts. When you fight for the milliseconds this can make the difference between who is first to finish and win.

When your reaction time is good you keep up with your opponent and the demands of the game, eventually frustrating your opponent into getting impatient and making errors. You can exploit this in order to win the point (or basket, try or goal) and ultimately the fixture.

Negative impacts on performance

When your reaction time is a development need you will take a long time to make a decision and act upon that decision. This will negatively impact on your performance as your opponent can get free of you and into a strong attacking position in the time that it takes for you to act. In directly competitive activities this is a disadvantage as your ultimate aim is to deny your opponent space and time. This will result in you allowing them the upper hand and them eventually scoring the point (or basket, try or goal) and that may lead to them winning the fixture.

In racing activities if you are excited your reaction time may be affected if you are too quick and perform a false start. This would result in you being even slower to start the next time, for fear of doing the same again, or being automatically disqualified as is the case in some activities these days.

DON'T FORGET

Reaction time is shorter when you are at the automatic stage of learning. This is due to quicker information-processing and decision-making.

ONLINE TEST

Test yourself on this topic at www.brightredbooks.net

THINGS TO DO AND THINK ABOUT

1 Complete the table below where explanations are given for how agility impacts on performance. Analyse the explanation and tick whether it is describing a positive or negative impact on performance. Write down what activity is being described.

EXPLANATION OF THE IMPACT OF AGILITY ON PERFORMANCE	POSITIVE	NEGATIVE	ACTIVITY
My agility helps me to turn quickly to avoid being tackled by defenders, maintain my balance, move quickly and make decisions fast.			
I am unable to get down into low positions so that I can dig the ball and return it effectively because I have weak legs and I lack flexibility.			
I cannot save shots that come to me on my left side as I am not agile enough to move quickly and get my body behind the ball.			
My agility means that I move at speed with grace. This helps me to complete complex tumbling routines and score highly from the judges.			

2 How does agility impact on your performance in an activity of your own choice? In your answer, make sure you:
  - provide a definition of agility
  - state your position within the activity of your choice
  - explain in detail how agility positively impacts on your performance
  - explain in detail how agility can negatively impact on your performance.

3 How does reaction time impact on your performance in an activity of your own choice? In your answer, make sure you:
  - provide a definition of reaction time
  - state your position within the activity of your choice
  - explain in detail how reaction time positively impacts on your performance
  - explain in detail how reaction time can negatively impact on your performance.

4 Explain these two factors and how they impact on your performance to a family member or friend. Try not to look at your notes. Encourage them to ask questions such as 'why', 'how' and 'can you give another example?'.

SKILL-RELATED: BALANCE

Balance is the ability to retain your centre of gravity above your base of support without falling over. You can retain balance when you are stationary (static balance) or when you are moving (dynamic balance).

- **Static balance** is the ability to maintain your control or position whilst remaining stationary.
- **Dynamic balance** is the ability to maintain balance and control of the body whilst moving.

When performers are balanced their body tension allows them to maintain control of their body as it is moving and changing into different positions and shapes. Performers have to ensure that they have an even distribution of weight to allow them to remain upright, steady and in control of their body as they perform their skills and techniques.

DON'T FORGET

Balance is essential in all activities as movement is key to physical performance.

VIDEO LINK

Watch the following clip demonstrating exceptional dynamic and static balance. Please remember these are trained professionals and you should not try this yourself. Watch this to see why.

ONLINE TEST

Head to www.brightredbooks.net to test your knowledge of the fitness factors which impact on performance.

ONLINE

For more sample answers like the one in Question 3, head to www.brightredbooks.net

ONLINE

Visit www.brightredbooks.net to read about core stability as another sub factor of physical skill related fitness.

POSITIVE IMPACTS ON PERFORMANCE

Balance can positively impact on your performance in subjective activities as it allows you to maintain control of your body both whilst moving or static. Having good balance and control of all movements will ensure that performers score highly from the judges and perform to their best.

In directly competitive activities, performers need balance to continually move and adjust their body position when trying to mark an opponent, when looking for space or when trying to create scoring opportunities. Good balance will help these players keep their shots on target, to maintain possession when being pushed by defenders and to recover quickly in order to prepare for their next movement.

NEGATIVE IMPACTS ON PERFORMANCE

In aesthetic activities, your routine is compromised when you lack static balance and when you cannot perform complex skills and techniques. Without balance you would lose control of your body position and tension whilst in the air and this would negatively impact on your landing. This would result in you scoring fewer points from the judges and finishing lower than you would like.

In directly competitive activities when dynamic balance is weak we are unable to move efficiently around our playing area whilst performing our various skills and techniques. When a performer has a base of support that is small and immobile they will struggle to retain their centre of gravity above this base and transfer their weight when required. This could result in them stumbling or failing to get any power into their skills or techniques, both of which will negatively affect the outcome of their performance.

THINGS TO DO AND THINK ABOUT

1 Look at the pictures below and tick whether they demonstrate static or dynamic balance. Explain why.

EXAMPLE	STATIC	DYNAMIC
(ballet dancer)		
(pole vaulter)		
(rugby players)		
(boxers)		

2 How does balance impact on your performance in an activity of your own choice? In your answer, make sure you:
- provide a definition of balance
- explain in detail how balance positively impacts on your performance
- explain in detail how balance can negatively impact on your performance.

3 Look at the sample of model answer below. Analyse the responses and suggest a physical or skill-related sub-factor that is being described.

When _____ is good you will be able to propel yourself in the direction you are travelling as you row. Your technique will be effective and this will result in you conserving energy early on in your performance. The _____ you can generate in each stroke will result in you fatiguing as you maintain your position alongside other competitors before you can exert your conserved energy in the sprint finish.

4 Read back through the answers you have given throughout this chapter and try to expand further on the positive and negative impacts.

5 Provide another example from the same activity to demonstrate how this factor can impact positively or negatively. Ask yourself whether you have justified what you have written and consider exactly how it helps your overall performance. It might help to discuss and get feedback from classmates, teachers, parents or carers.

 DON'T FORGET

Similarly to types of strength, there are two types of balance. **Static** (remaining still) and **dynamic** (on the move).

SKILL QUALITIES: TIMING AND RHYTHM

Skill quality relates to many features of a performer's skill repertoire. These features can be split into three categories as shown in the table.

TECHNICAL QUALITIES	SPECIAL QUALITIES	QUALITY OF PERFORMANCE	
• timing • rhythm • consistency	• creativity	• accuracy • control	• fluency • effort

In this section we will look at timing, rhythm, creativity, imagination, accuracy and control, but as you can see there are a number of other relevant technical qualities.

DON'T FORGET

Timing can be the combination of decision-making, co-ordination and reaction time.

DON'T FORGET

In team invasion games, timing is essential in both attacking and defensive play.

TECHNICAL QUALITY: TIMING

Impact on performance

Timing is the choice, judgement, or control of when something should be done. It is the ability to coincide movements in relation to external factors. Combining decision-making, co-ordination and reaction time successfully will get the performer in the right place at the right time. Timing is involved in all activities. For example, in dance or gymnastics the performer should time their movements to be in time with the beat or tempo of music, and in netball you must judge the speed of your teammates move in order to give an accurately timed pass for them to move onto.

Positive impacts on performance

Having good timing in an activity will enable the performer to be in the right place at the right time. They will have decided where to move, when to move and how quickly this needs to be carried out. They will have considered the movements that will be executed and they will consider others around them, such as the involvement of team-mates or opposition positioning. Good timing means they either arrive at the required place on the pitch or court with time to spare (more time to make decisions) or they arrive at the exact time required. For example, when jumping to hit a spike, the timing of the jump is crucial in order to contact the ball at its highest point. This will ensure you successfully perform the skill.

Negative impacts on performance

When a performer has poor timing they will fail to reach their desired position at the correct time. This could result in them being unable to execute their skill, such as missing a pass from a team-mate or not landing a somersault in gymnastics as they have rotated too late.

TECHNICAL QUALITY: RHYTHM

Rhythm is the expression of timing during the performance of a skill or movement. The ability to coordinate the body during a movement at the correct time can also define rhythm. In athletics a triple jumper needs good rhythm. They must coordinate their run up, take off (from the board), the hop and step phases and the jumping phase. Each phase requires different movement speeds that must combine into a rhythmic pattern.

Positive impacts on performance

Having rhythm will enable a performer to move to good time within a performance. They will be able to form a movement pattern by co-ordinating their body to move at the correct speed and tempo. This can be done as an individual or as a team.

Negative impacts on performance

When a performer has poor rhythm their performance will look disjointed and awkward. They will be unable to perform their skill or sequence due to poor timing and a lack of co-ordinating their body within the correct space.

 ACTIVITY

1   Generate examples for how timing could have a positive and negative effect on your performance in an individual activity of your choice.

2   Using this example, can you think of a time when rhythm has impacted positively and negatively on your performance?

HINT: Remember to say what happened and more importantly what difference this made to your performance.

THINGS TO DO AND THINK ABOUT

1   In an activity of your choice explain how consistent you are and why.

2   In the same activity give examples of when rhythm and timing are evident in your performance. Remember to explain how and why.

 ONLINE

Visit www.brightredbooks.net to read about consistency and how it impacts on performance.
HINT: Be precise to your chosen activity. Think of real game scenarios to help you add specific detail.

 DON'T FORGET

You can be consistently bad in a performance as well as consistently good. Make sure your answers are clear about this. Rhythm and timing are both closely linked. However, timing is when something should be done and rhythm is the expression of the timing (or the doing of it).

 ONLINE

See a model answer for this question at www.brightredbooks.net

 ONLINE

Test yourself on skill qualities at www.brightredbooks.net

SPECIAL QUALITIES AND QUALITY OF PERFORMANCE

SPECIAL QUALITY: CREATIVITY

To be creative within a performance is to be unique, inventive or unusual and ultimately different from the norm. A creative individual in a sporting context will be aware of what is going on around them. They will understand their own strengths and weaknesses and whether or not they have the ability to create this new skill, movement or tactic. They will also be judging their teammates involvement and that of the opposition. For example, in netball, a wing attack feeding the ball into their shooting circle must be creative on the ball to confuse the defender, for example by looking to the right and passing the ball to the left (faking).

Positive impacts on performance

A performer with creativity will be able to outwit their opponents. They will perform the unexpected and make it difficult for opponents to predict what they will do next. This may result in them winning more points. For example, a creative dance routine will impress the judges and they may receive more points.

Negative impacts on performance

A performer with a lack of creativity will struggle to think of what to do next. When they are placed in challenging contexts they may find it difficult to use their imagination to get them out of trouble. For example, in netball when you have a very tall defender in front of you that you cannot see passed and you have three seconds to pass the ball, you could become nervous and be unsure of what to do. This will result in a foul and the opposition will gain possession.

ONLINE

See an example of how creativity can positively or negatively impact on performance at www.brightredbooks.net

DON'T FORGET

Creativity can also be explained as an ability to demonstrate the element of surprise.

QUALITY OF PERFORMANCE: ACCURACY

To be accurate in sporting terms is the ability to direct an object to a desired target or to carry out a particular movement with precision. For example, in tennis, serving the ball into the corner of the service box and onto your opponents' backhand requires a high degree of accuracy. In gymnastics, a performer producing a complex routine to a high standard can be described as being accurate in terms of their skills being performed precisely.

Positive impacts on performance

Having accuracy in your performance means that you can put your body or an object exactly where you want it. Movements will be executed with complete control displaying quality timing, flow, technique etc. When an object is involved and is to be thrown, kicked or struck, a performer will be able to judge the height, speed and direction of it and will control their limbs to accurately pinpoint its destination.

contd

Negative impacts on performance

Movements that lack accuracy will display poor technique. For example, a performer may rotate too early or too late, causing them to fall as they have not accurately performed the technique. Where an object is used, the performer will be unable to place the object into the correct area, such as a tennis serve into the service box. This would cause double faults and the opposition receiving points.

QUALITY OF PERFORMANCE: CONTROL

A performer described as having control has the ability to manage their body. They will be self-aware in knowing what is required from their trunk and limbs in order to carry out certain movements.

Body management is crucial in all sports. For example, in gymnastics, core stability provides the base of support from which to execute skills. Other examples come from sports where objects are involved. There are two types of object control:

- **propulsive** - sending an object away (throwing, kicking, striking, batting)

- **receptive** - receiving an object (catching, dribbling a ball, receiving a shuttlecock).

Propulsive skills can be considered slightly easier to execute because it is easier to control the object that you are sending. Receptive skills can be considered more difficult due to the movements involved before receiving such objects (perceptual and co-ordination skills).

Positive impacts on performance

Having control within your performances will help you manage your body in order to execute simple and complex skills to a high standard. Performances will look better and technique will be effective.

Negative impacts on performance

A performer who lacks control will struggle to perform skills effectively. Their performance may also look unorganised as their timing and accuracy will be negatively impacted.

THINGS TO DO AND THINK ABOUT

1 Select an activity of your choice.

   (a) Explain how a lack of creativity could impact your performance in this activity.

   (b) Explain how having a good level of control can impact on your performance in your chosen activity.

   (c) Analyse how accuracy impacts on your performance in your chosen activity.

DON'T FORGET

Control, accuracy and creativity all contribute towards the quality of a performance. A performance can be deemed unsuccessful where control, accuracy and creativity do not exist.

DON'T FORGET

There are two types of object control: propulsive (when sending an object away from you) and receptive (when you receive an object).

ONLINE

Watch the two clips at www.brightredbooks.net and see which performance is the most successful in terms of the quality of it.

ONLINE TEST

Test yourself on skill qualities at www.brightredbooks.net

TACTICAL PERFORMANCE CONSIDERATIONS

DON'T FORGET

Tactics are predominately necessary in directly competitive activities where your competitor has a direct impact on how you perform.

INTRODUCTION

Tactics are actions or strategies that are planned to achieve a specific outcome. For athletes this outcome means that they outwit and defeat their competitors.

When planning your winning tactics you need to consider a number of sub-factors. These sub-factors can be separated into two categories:

- performance considerations
- principles of play.

Performance considerations deal with the demands of the game, including your role, the conditions, history and your own and your opponent's strengths and weaknesses.

The principles of play are concerned with the set strategies or systems that performers must adhere to. If they understand why the principles and performance considerations are in place, then they should be able to apply these principles and considerations in new and unfamiliar situations.

DON'T FORGET

Within your course you may have studied other sub-factors that will also fall into the physical tactical factor category.

PERFORMANCE CONSIDERATIONS	PRINCIPLES OF PLAY
Personal strengths and weaknesses team strengths and weaknesses	Width
Demands of your role	Depth
	Delay

STRENGTHS AND WEAKNESSES

Strengths and weaknesses are the mental, emotional, social and physical attributes of an individual or a collective team. They can be deemed a strength or weakness of their performance based on how these factors impact on their performance. Successful performers or teams will highlight and play to their strengths during their performance. At the same time they will work hard to hide and combat any weaknesses that they may have.

Positive impacts on performance

It is important to devise a tactic or plan which maximises your own strengths and minimises your weaknesses. If you are tall and strong you should plan tactics that highlight this strength, such as the use of crosses into the box in football. Alternatively, if you are a quick player with good technical skills, you would benefit from playing a fast passing and moving game. Coaches and players need to work together before competitions to tactically plan how to highlight the performer's strengths. This will set the players up to help them play their best and defeat their opponents, even if the opponents may be technically stronger. The tactics are the key to undoing strong opponents and getting tactics right will ensure you outwit your opponents and win the fixture.

Negative impacts on performance

Your opponents' strengths could have a negative impact on your performance if they have an influential player who you are struggling to contain. For example, when defending against a team who has a high floating striker, it may not be clear who is responsible for defending them as they move between various zones. Your defenders need to choose whether to mark closely and stray out of their own position, or stay and communicate to a team-mate that the striker is in their zone. A clear understanding of what each member of the team needs to do to counteract the opposition tactics is essential.

THINGS TO DO AND THINK ABOUT

1 List your personal strengths. What unique attributes do you bring to your performance?

2 Explain how the tactics, strategies or compositions you perform suit your personal strengths.

3 State what weaknesses you may have when you are performing.

4 Explain what you plan to do to combat or hide this weakness during competition.

ROLE DEMANDS

Your role is the part you play in your chosen activity. In a team game, you will probably have more than one role. For example, your position is one role, but you may have other roles as team captain, and as the person responsible for taking free kicks and penalties. Certain qualities are required to fulfil the performance demands of each individual role, and your unique attributes should dictate your best role. For teams to be successful, performers need to meet the demands of their individual role, so that the team can meet the demands of the competition.

DON'T FORGET

Role demands are similar to your role and responsibilities with the social factor.

VIDEO LINK

Watch penalty corners being executed in the European Hockey League at www.brightredbooks.net

DON'T FORGET

Having individuals with different strengths who have different roles will ensure a team or group have more combined strengths.

POSITIVE IMPACTS ON PERFORMANCE

Role demands relate to your own personal strengths and weaknesses and the role that you are asked to complete during your performance. For example, in hockey, the corner injector has to deliver the ball quickly and accurately during a corner. Our quick and brave players are post runners, as they have to get themselves into a positive scoring position to score a deflection, or be a decoy to encourage the defenders to come out of their area to mark them, creating space in front of the goal. Our stopper stops the ball as quickly and efficiently as possible, for our striker to quickly shoot the ball at the goal or to a runner at the post. Then there is a slip player, who may be used as a passing option to the right or the left. Every player will practice their unique role over and over again to ensure that it is automatic and they are prepared for a variety of situations that may occur. This happens in training and the most consistent players are then given the role in the game. For us to score the corner everyone has to perform their individual role quickly and effectively so that we can utilise all of our options and exploit the opportunity we have in a dangerous area.

NEGATIVE IMPACTS ON PERFORMANCE

Role demands could have a negative impact on your performance if it highlights your weakness as opposed to combating it. For example in aesthetic activities it would be detrimental to the group performance if the person you asked to be the base of a group balance was not very strong. The job of being at the base of a group balance requires static strength, concentration and control. When the base is shaky and instable then this will affect the rest of the group as they perform their own balances. If they were not able to perform their role at the correct moment with confidence and self-assurance then their group members would begin to sense their apprehension and would also feel less confident as a result.

DON'T FORGET

The strength of the team as a whole is dependent on each individual effectively performing their role.

 THINGS TO DO AND THINK ABOUT

1 Complete the table to outline the role of particular performers.

ROLE	ROLE DEMANDS
Goalkeeper	Protect the goal, make saves, communicate to defenders, take goal kicks
Spiker (volleyball)	
	Ball handler, call set plays, pass and move quickly, take 3 pointers
Male ice-skater in pair	
	Stay outside the circles, defend and support attack, take centre pass
Scrum Half	

2 (a) State your preferred role within your chosen activity.

(b) Explain what you individually have responsibility for doing.

(c) Describe why this is essential to a successful performance in your group or team.

ONLINE

Complete the SWOT analysis at www.brightredbooks.net to help you think about your strengths and weaknesses.

ONLINE TEST

Complete the online test at www.brightredbooks.net

TACTICAL PRINCIPLES OF PLAY: WIDTH

INTRODUCTION

Tactically there are a number of principles of play that occur in attack and defence that can help players. When players understand the general principles of the tactics they are using then they will be able to transfer this knowledge and apply it to a variety of different situations as they occur. Team games are directly competitive and played in an open environment, so it is very difficult to predict the exact types of situations that will occur, but by understanding a number of principles of plays, performers will be better placed to adapt and use the guidelines outlined within the principles.

DON'T FORGET

Width means making full use of the whole width of the playing area.

WIDTH

The principle of **width** can be described as having a spread of players across the whole playing area, to cover the full breadth of the pitch, court or field. In many team invasive games the middle channel is where the majority of play occurs, but teams that can exploit the space left by their opponents out wide can find a way of getting in behind teams and creating scoring opportunities. Applying width in attack means that you pass the ball wide, with the intention of getting space and time to cross the ball into a scoring position. Or if the defender starts to come out to this player then it creates gaps in their zone for your teammates to penetrate and exploit. This creates scoring opportunities.

Positive impacts on performance

When players can stretch the pitch and hold their position then they will be able to utilise the full breadth of space available to them. Defenders would love nothing more than for teams to play down the middle channel, as this makes their job easy. When teams play width in attack, players attack the space out wide that is available to them and move the defenders out of their comfortable position. This generates more time on the ball and makes it easier to make good decisions about the best options. Applying width in attack makes defenders work much harder to cover more space and the overall effect is to create more scoring opportunities.

VIDEO LINK

Watch the clip showing teams using width in attack at www.brightredbooks.net

Negative impacts on performance

In field sports with centrally positioned goals or nets, width in attack can negatively impact on performance. The space out wide is not in a very dangerous area, and if the defenders do not come out of their zone to pressurise the attackers, then the attackers may have possession but it is in a weak position which is difficult to score from directly. Without suitable skills to make and use good crosses, the principle of width does not help create scoring opportunities.

DON'T FORGET

Applying the principle of width takes discipline and patience as you hold your position and shape.

DON'T FORGET

Width is predominantly required in team invasive games, where you need to exploit an area that your opponents need to defend.

 THINGS TO DO AND THINK ABOUT

1 Look at the performance situations stated below and think of a tactic that would positively respond to this situation.

PERFORMANCE SITUATION	TACTICAL RESPONSE
Opponent has a weak backhand.	
You're losing, it's the last 5 minutes of game.	
You are a fast finisher in a race.	
You have strong, tall attackers.	
It is windy and the ground is muddy.	
An influential player is injured.	

2 Complete the SWOT analysis at www.brightredbooks.net to help you think about the tactics that you play and analyse them critically. An example below has been completed for you regarding zone defence.

STRENGTHS – Zone Defence	WEAKNESSES – Zone Defence
Protects the key area from penetrating runs.	Requires lots of communication and co-operation.
Shares the responsibility for defending.	If one player does not do job it will fail.
Less physically demanding.	Does not prevent outside shots.
OPPORTUNITIES – Zone Defence	**THREATS – Zone Defence**
Can delay attacks and slow the game down.	Gives your opponents possession.
Great position to break fast from.	Seams between zones can be exposed.
Invites low percentage shots you can rebound.	Allows outside shots.

DON'T FORGET

Width will have limited effectiveness if crossing is not a strength of a teams performance.

ONLINE TEST

Complete the online test at www.brightredbooks.net

TACTICAL PRINCIPLES OF PLAY: DEPTH

The principle of **depth** involves having a player further back than the others so that they can be utilised in either defence or attack. Depth can be defined in performance terms as the distance from the top to the bottom of a structure or composition. When depth is applied there would always be a player deeper than the rest in defence to act as cover, whilst in attack there would be opportunities to pass back in order to retain possession or begin to transfer the ball to the opposite side of play. Depth is a supportive principle that ensures the player on or nearest to the ball has help and assistance deeper on their pitch, court or field.

POSITIVE IMPACTS ON PERFORMANCE

Depth in defence can impact on your performance positively by allowing a defending team to have a sweeper who can mop up and cover any defensive mistakes. It is like having another line of defence. When applying depth in attack it is useful to have a player deeper than everyone else in order to help keep possession of the ball and reorganise and attack down a different channel. A player may also come from deep to receive a weighted pass and create an overload of players in a particular part of the pitch.

Negative impacts on performance

Depth could negatively impact on your performance because if your opponents apply depth against you then they may create overload in attack. When a defender is encouraged to come up and support an attack then this presents our defence with the added challenge of trying to mark an additional player. This attack maybe spontaneous and if so we will be caught unaware and left with an overload of players to defend. In this situation our opposition had the upper hand as they had more options than we can defend against. Similarly our opponents comfortably transitioned the ball across the back after passing to their sweeper who quickly releases a fast pass across the pitch. This was difficult for us as we had to quickly respond, reshape and get across to put pressure on them as they attacked the opposite channel. When they did this to us a few times our concentration faded as our fitness levels were exposed and we became slower to respond. This allowed them to have more time and space to score the chances they created.

DON'T FORGET

Depth means making the playing area as long as possible and having cover or support deeper than the ball.

VIDEO LINK

Watch the clip showing Barcelona maintaining possession of the ball by applying the principle of depth in attack at www.brightredbooks.net. Count how many passes they make in the clip. Now count how many of these passes are backward.

VIDEO LINK

Watch the clip showing a volleyball attack that applies depth at www.brightredbooks.net. Ask yourself which player spikes the ball and where have they come from.

ACTIVITY

Read the model answers below and fill in the blanks.

Select from: Width, Strengths, Role, Weakness, Delay.

"If you are a powerful badminton player and have an effective overhead clear and your opponent does not, then a sensible tactic would be to try to force your opponent to the back of their court using your overhead clear. This will force them to play a weak return that you can attack with a smash. Playing them to the back of their court will place them in a defensive position it highlights your _____ whilst exploiting your opponents _____."

"In basketball our team _____ is our fitness, our skill level deteriorates towards the end of the game and we make mistakes. This is because our average team cardio-vascular endurance is only in the average category of the national norms table. To combat this _____ we tactically play a zone defence for the majority of the game, so that we can conserve energy and share the defensive responsibility throughout the team."

"In golf I apply the principle of _____ by trying to take as long as I can to walk up the fairway to play my next shot. This is because the wind direction and speed had picked up and I was hoping to play my shot when it had died down again. By taking my time and _____ my shot I was trying to give myself the best possible chance to play my shot accurately and onto the green."

"In the 5000m my individual _____ are that I am a fast finisher, as I have excellent speed endurance. Therefore the tactics I plan involve staying in a good position in the leading pack in the race. Ideally I would look to remain in behind a competitor in order that I can conserve some energy by being in their slip stream. With the view to pull out with 300m remaining and allowing my fast finish to win the race for me."

"In basketball, _____ is an important principle of our play. We need to find space in our opponents' key as we aim to score. Therefore, we invade their half of the court and use the _____ of the court when attacking. This pulls our opponents out of their defensive positions in the key. The space that is then left can be exploited by our attackers to create more scoring opportunities."

THINGS TO DO AND THINK ABOUT

1   Describe and explain a tactical principle of play in an activity of your choosing. In your answer, make sure you give:
    - a definition of the principle of play
    - an explanation of how it could positively impact on your performance
    - an explanation of how it could negatively impact on your performance.

2   Read through your answer and try to expand further on the positive and negative impacts. Provide another example from the same activity to demonstrate how this factor can impact positively or negatively. (Have you justified what you have stated, how exactly does it help your overall performance?)

3   Repeat Questions 1 and 2 with another principle of play.

4   Explain these two tactical principles and how they impact on your performance to a family member or friend. Try not to look at your notes. Encourage them to ask questions such as 'why', 'how' and 'can you give another example?'.

 ONLINE

Visit www.brightredbooks.net to read about delay as another tactical factor and how it impacts on performance.

DON'T FORGET

You can have depth in defence and also depth in attack.

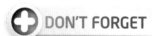 DON'T FORGET

In preparation for the exam you should know about at least two of these social sub-factors in depth.

 ONLINE

Find an extension to this activity at www.brightredbooks.net

 ONLINE TEST

Complete the online test at www.brightredbooks.net

METHODS OF GATHERING INFORMATION TO ANALYSE PERFORMANCE

INTRODUCTION

WHY DO WE COLLECT INFORMATION ON OUR PERFORMANCE?

We collect information on performance to:

- identify performance **strengths and weaknesses**, in order to plan the next appropriate course of action

- identify **specific performance requirements** for activities, in order to apply specific training approaches needed to improve performance

- help to collect information that will provide **accurate, valid and reliable results**

- set an appropriate **starting point** for a training programme

- help **set appropriate goals** (targets) within a development programme which are **realistic**, **challenging** and **achievable**

- provide data and results that can be used as a benchmark (baseline data) that can be **compared against at a later date to monitor progress** and **identify improvements**

- provide the means to monitor the effectiveness of a training programme. This will help you to make an **evidence-based decision** on whether to change your development programme if required.

 DON'T FORGET

It is important that you know the reasons outlined above as you may be asked to **explain**, **analyse** or **evaluate** why you selected certain methods of gathering information.

 DON'T FORGET

You collect information so that you can make a more informed plan to improve and develop performance.

RELIABILITY, VALIDITY, PRACTICALITY

All tests, observation schedules, questionnaires or data gathered has to be:
- valid
- reliable
- practical
- measurable.

If it is all these things then it will stand up to scrutiny and accurately provide trustworthy data. The validity and reliability of qualitative data is bound by the honesty, impartiality and level of experience of the person or persons providing the opinions or observations used to generate the data.

In order for your method of collecting information to be reliable, valid and practical you need to consider if it:
- is appropriate to the factor or sub-factor you are gathering information on
- provides definitive quantitative or qualitative information

 DON'T FORGET

When you are asked to analyse, you should identify at least two aspects of each method and analyse the relationship between the aspect and the factor impacting on performance.

contd

- is simple enough for you to conduct and analyse in class
- is fit for purpose and working appropriately (video technology, HRM etc)
- can be conducted during competitive performance (this is preferable and more valid and reliable than during practice)
- can be conducted under exactly the same conditions every time (same venue, time of day, equipment, by the same person)
- fits into your PDP at the appropriate time (before, during and after, spread out evenly)
- is a nationally recognised test with quality assured national norms results.

Any technology used should be chosen to help the accuracy of your analysis. For example, video can be stopped, started or rewound, numerical data can be plotted on graphs, specialist software such as *Dartfish* can visually compare you to a top performer in your chosen sport.

APPLICABLE TESTS AND ANALYTICAL TOOLS TO COLLECT INFORMATION

There are many different ways to collect information. Some methods are specific only to certain factors, whereas other methods can be used to gather information on various factors.

This table outline the methods to gather information on the different factors that we will cover in this chapter.

PHYSICAL			MENTAL	EMOTIONAL	SOCIAL
FITNESS	SKILLS	TACTICS			
Standardised tests	Match Observation Schedule	Game Statistics League Tables	SCAT test	Profile Wheel	Questionnaire
General Obs Schedule	Movement Analysis Schedule	Team Feedback Meeting	Mental Performance Evaluation	Sport Emotion Questionnaire	
Match Analysis Table	Scattergraph	Tactical Obs Schedule	Video Analysis	Emotional Control Record	Coach Feedback
Timed Obs Schedule	Video Analysis	Video Analysis		Video Analysis	Video Analysis

Visit www.brightredbooks.net and look at the example answers on gathering data. Analyse the answer and identify what method of gathering information is being described.

 THINGS TO DO AND THINK ABOUT

Look at the table above and identify what methods are appropriate for your activity and the factors you are planning to develop.

 **DON'T FORGET**

The list in the table is not exhaustive. You may have covered a different method in your course that you will prefer to discuss.

 **DON'T FORGET**

Similar methods of gathering information are applicable in a few factors. Knowing how to describe these methods will ensure that you can answer a wider variety of questions during your exam.

 VIDEO LINK

Check out the clip at www.brightredbooks.net for more on reviewing information from performance.

 ONLINE TEST

Test yourself on gathering information online at www.brightredbooks.net

PLANNING AND PREPARING FOR PERFORMANCE

CHALLENGES

When planning for your performance it is vital that performers understand that challenges will arise that may impact on their performance. If you consider these challenges then you will be ready to face them and perform to your best. The challenges you face will impact on the **physical, social, mental** and **emotional** factors. In this chapter the aim is to learn how to apply knowledge of these factors to your understanding of how different challenges can impact on your performance within your chosen activity.

DON'T FORGET

The challenge is linked to a factor that impacts on performance. This will help you identify a suitable performance development plan.

Preparation for your single performance involves:
- identifying factors that impact on performance
- understanding the potential impact on performance
- identifying challenges faced by a performer
- planning and preparing for performance
- Implementing a performance development plan.

As a performer you will face a number of challenges that differ within activities. A list of some of the potential challenges and the factors they influence is shown in the table.

CHALLENGE	FACTOR	EXPLANATION
Weather	Social (environment)	Temperature, wind, rain, snow and ice all affect outdoor activities.
Previous losses	Mental (mental toughness)	Being on a losing streak or having a poor record against some teams could impact on your belief.
Injury	Physical (fitness)	Being hurt means that you have to play differently to combat your weakness.
Fear	Emotional (fear)	When overly anxious about a competition you may lack self-belief and you cannot perform your best.
Crowd	Social (audience) Mental (concentration)	Having an audience can affect your ability to focus and concentrate on your role.
Winning	Physical (tactics)	When winning you have to ensure you protect your lead and deny your opponents chances.
Trust	Emotional	Having trust will affect your confidence as you believe in every member of your team.

DON'T FORGET

Some challenges may only affect you individually, such as nerves or injury, whilst other challenges may affect your whole team, such as weather conditions and changing tactics.

By working through some of these problems and considering how you would act and adapt in order to combat the challenge, you will be better placed to deal with them if they occur during your single performance. They all affect the decisions that you need to make regarding your selection of tactics, compositions and skills.

Planning for performance

1. **(a) Explain the relevance of the <u>two challenges</u> you will face in this single performance** (4)
- You need to get this part right (choose challenges wisely) otherwise you will make things difficult for yourself in the questions that follow (and lose marks!)
- Two marks are available for explaining each challenge
- Challenges must be related to your chosen single (one-off) performance
- Challenges can relate to any of the four factors

DON'T FORGET

Planning effectively in this stage will also help you to analyse and answer the scenario performance problem in Section 2 of your final exam.

contd

What are challenges?

A challenge is something you will be faced with in your one-off performance that you will try to overcome. When planning for your performance, it is vital that you understand that challenges will arise that may impact on your performance. If you consider these challenges then you will be ready to face them and perform to your best. They will be impacted by Physical, Social, Mental and Emotional factors. In part (a) you need to show that you can apply knowledge of these factors to your understanding of how different challenges can impact on your performance within your chosen activity.

Selecting (the right) challenges

Choose two challenges from two different factors. Why? Well, this will enable you to broaden your answer. You will have more information to select from and to use in your answer. Therefore you should be able to gain marks more easily.

Be realistic and specific to you! Place yourself on that playing area and consider anything that 'concerns' you about this single one-off performance.

Answering the questions

Think about the command words. What do they mean?

When **explaining** your challenges, have you:
1. Said clearly what your challenges are?
2. Explained why each challenge **is** a challenge for you?
3. Given two points (for each challenge) that explain the relevance of the challenges to you in this one-off performance?

1. **(b) Identify the actions you will take to meet each of the challenges in 1 (a). Explain why these actions are appropriate.** **(4 marks)**
- There must be a clear relationship between the challenges and the <u>appropriateness</u> of the actions taken
- What is the **command word**? What is the question asking?
- How many marks do you think are available for identifying the actions you will take? None!
- Aim for two marks per challenge (although you can also get a 3/1 mark split!)
- For each challenge give a minimum of two points of explanation for the appropriateness of your actions.

Evaluation of performance

Q3 (a) Analyse the effectiveness of your preparation for the two challenges explained in 1(a). **6 marks**

You are being asked to **analyse** how effective the preparation for your challenges was. So, you are analysing your answer from Q1(b).

You must relate your answer to the challenges, e.g.
– Did the preparation help? If so, how? If not, why?

Once you state what the impact on performance was after carrying out your preparation, you will be able to answer this question.

Q3 (b) Evaluate at least one strength of, and at least one area for development from, your performance. **6 marks**

Note the command word – **evaluate**. Base your evaluation on some of the following:
- Quantitative: scores, time, height, distance or personal best
- Qualitative: feelings of success, emotional responses, mood, pressure felt

Choose different strengths and development needs from anything else mentioned previously. This should stop you repeating yourself and give you more to talk about.

You may want to give **more than one** strength and **more than one** development need to give yourself a better chance of gaining all 6 marks.

ONLINE

Visit www.brightredbooks.net for more help understanding the question and more examples of potential challenges.

DON'T FORGET

You must make clear the relationship between the single performance and each challenge. (Challenges can be Mental, Emotional, Social or Physical.)

ONLINE

See the online examples (1–4) of some model answers and the marks that could be allocated to them at www.brightredbooks.net

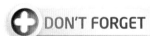

DON'T FORGET

Marks will be awarded up to 2 marks for each challenge, so if you only explain one in depth you will only be eligible for 2 of the 4 marks available.

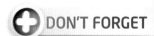

DON'T FORGET

Your explanation must make clear the relationship between the challenges and the preparation required.

PERFORMANCE AND EVALUATING PERFORMANC

PERFORMANCE

40% of your marks for Higher Physical Education will come from the single performance. You will be observed during this performance and allocated marks based on the criteria shown in the table. It is important that you understand these criteria and try to make sure you meet them during your performance.

Assessment criteria

Overview of mark allocation for Section 2

ASSESSMENT ITEM	0 MARKS	1–2 MARKS	3–4 MARKS	5–6 MARKS	7–8 MARKS
2 (a) Performance repertoire	Shows no evidence of a basic performance repertoire.	Applies a basic performance repertoire consistently.	Applies a **broad** performance repertoire, selecting and combining some complex skills appropriately to meet the demands of the performance context.	Applies a broad and **well established** performance repertoire, selecting and combining some complex skills **effectively** to meet the demands of the performance context.	Applies a broad and well established performance repertoire **consistently**, selecting and combining complex skills effectively to meet the demands of the performance context.
2 (b) Control and fluency	Shows no evidence of control and fluency during the performance.	Control and fluency usually demonstrated during the performance, while unchallenged.	Control and fluency usually demonstrated during the performance while responding with **variable effectiveness** to challenges.	Control and fluency usually demonstrated during the performance while responding **effectively** to challenges.	Control and fluency **consistently** demonstrated during the performance while responding effectively to challenges.
2 (c) Decision-making and problem solving throughout the performance	Shows no evidence of appropriate decision-making skills.	Demonstrates appropriate decision-making skills in response to a range of straightforward performance demands, throughout the performance.	Demonstrates **appropriate decision-making** skills in response to a range of challenging performance demands, throughout the performance.	Demonstrates ability to make appropriate decisions **quickly** in response to a range of challenging performance demands, throughout the performance.	Demonstrates ability to **anticipate** and make appropriate decisions quickly in response to a range of challenging performance demands, throughout the performance.
2 (d) The effectiveness of following through on the decision-making	Shows no evidence of effectiveness of following through on the decision-making during the performance.	Following through on decision-making results in limited effectiveness occasionally during the performance.	Following through on decision-making results in **limited effectiveness throughout** the performance.	Following through on decision-making results in **effectiveness throughout** the performance.	Following through on decision-making results in **effectiveness throughout** the performance, especially in response to **challenging demands**.
2 (e) Following rules and regulations and displaying etiquette during the performance	Shows no evidence of following rules and regulations or displaying appropriate etiquette.	Follows rules and regulations and displays appropriate etiquette occasionally during the performance.	Follows rules and regulations and displays appropriate etiquette at the start of, during, and at the end of the performance.		
2 (f) Control of emotions during the performance	Shows no evidence of controlling emotions during the performance.	Demonstrates control of emotions occasionally during the performance.	Demonstrates control of emotions throughout the performance.		

 ACTIVITY

Look at the clips of model performers at www.brightredbooks.net. Use the criteria shown in the table and award marks out of 40 for these single performances at Higher.

If you can, video your own performance and identify how you would score yourself under each of the headings. How can you improve or maintain this before your single performance?

EVALUATING PERFORMANCE

After your single performance you will be assessed on your ability to evaluate the effectiveness of their performance in relation to the planning and preparation carried out, the performance itself, and to provide an explanation of their future development needs. You will be asked to:

- review your performance
- evaluate performance strengths and areas for development
- identify future development needs.

The questions are shown in the table. 6 marks are allocated to each.

	QUESTION	mark
3 (a)	Analyse the effectiveness of your preparation for the two challenges explained in 1(a)	(6)
3 (b)	Evaluate at least one strength of, and at least one area for development, from your performance	(6)

 THINGS TO DO AND THINK ABOUT

Attempt to answer the questions yourself, from an activity of your choosing.

3 (a) Analyse the effectiveness of your preparation for the two challenges explained in 1(a). (6)

3 (b) Evaluate at least one strength of, and at least one area for development from, your performance. (6)

 DON'T FORGET

In 3(a) candidates can be awarded up to a maximum of 4 marks if they only describe one challenge, so make sure you analyse the effectiveness of both.
In 3(b) candidates can be awarded up to a maximum of 3 marks for an evaluation of a strength or an area for development. Therefore make sure you explain both to have access to all marks.

DON'T FORGET

Analytical points must relate the preparation undertaken in 1(b) to the effectiveness of how challenges were dealt with during the performance.

DON'T FORGET

Evaluation of performance can be based on the following criteria; quantitative scores, qualitative feelings, or any other relevant information. Evaluations must be backed up with reference to quantitative or qualitative analysis (facts or opinion).

ONLINE

Go to www.brightredbooks.net and do the activity on example answers for Q3(a) and (b).

DON'T FORGET

1 mark will be awarded for each analytical point about the effectiveness of preparation. It must link to 1(a).
1 mark will be allocated for each relevant point of evaluation, or for further development of this point.

DON'T FORGET

Preparation effectiveness must also link to your overall performance and assess whether this was successful or not.

GATHERING INFORMATION ON THE PHYSICAL FACTOR – FITNESS

ONLINE

Visit www.brightredbooks.net to view an example of an observation schedule on physical aspect of fitness.

DON'T FORGET

You will need to be able to **describe** the methods used to collect information. You will also need to be able **evaluate** one benefit and one limitation of using these method to collect information.

OBSERVATION SCHEDULES

An **observation schedule** gives a broad overview of your fitness levels within an activity. Once you have your results and have analysed your strengths and weaknesses you can look more closely using focused data at a specific aspect of your fitness. The headings in the example focus on 3 different games or matches but these headings can also be replaced by time intervals to give a timed phased observation schedule.

Benefits of using observation schedules

- Easy to complete in class by a peer.
- Results are easy to read and analyse afterwards.
- Can be adapted and made specific to different aspects (as above).
- Conducted during the game to give most accurate performance data.
- If used in conjunction with video analysis the information will be very reliable.

Limitations of using observation schedules

- You will need people of similar ability to play against.
- An observer is required who fully understands the criteria they are marking you against.
- Your observer must concentrate and pay attention throughout.
- Environmental issues (such as the weather) can impact on the performance.

STANDARDISED FITNESS TESTING

Standardised fitness testing is another important way to gather reliable information on physical fitness. There are numerous tests to select from and they will give good quality data and information that is **valid**, **reliable** and **objective**.

Validity

A valid test is one that provides useful and meaningful results, because it is measuring what it claims to measure. For each of the physical fitness sub-factors there is a valid standardised test.

Reliability

Reliability refers to the nature of how the tests have been carried out, especially in relation to repeated tests being carried out under the same conditions. To ensure **consistency** of results, tests should feature:

- the same performers
- the same playing conditions
- tests and analyses carried out in the same way
- results recorded in the same way.

For a test to be **reliable**, it must not be affected by the tester. This is important in fitness assessment and testing, where more than one person is carrying out the test.

contd

Objectivity

The **objectivity** can be increased by ensuring that equipment for measuring is accurate. There should be clearly defined procedures for testing and recording, which should be repeated each time the tests are carried out.

 ONLINE

Examples of standardised fitness tests can be found online at www.brightredbooks.net

Benefits of using standardised fitness tests

- Each test is specific to a particular aspect of fitness.
- Tests follow the same protocol, so each performer follows the same procedures.
- Tests are widely recognised.
- Norms are established.
- Tests provide a permanent record of results, can be repeated and compared at a later date.
- Results can be compared to elite or model performer.
- Results will be used to set the correct training intensity and goals.
- Strengths and weaknesses are identified.

Limitations of using standardised fitness tests

- Standard tests may require specific measuring equipment.
- Some testing could be expensive.
- If laboratory conditions are required, access to a laboratory may be difficult.
- Tests are not specific to the activity.

THINGS TO DO AND THINK ABOUT

Name an observation table that you have used during your course.	Description – give details of what it looks like and how you completed it.	State one benefit of using this method –
		State one limitation of using this method –
Name a standardised fitness test that you have used during your course.	Description – give details of what it looks like and how you completed it.	State one benefit of using this method –
		State one limitation of using this method –

 **ONLINE TEST**

Head to www.brightredbooks.net to test yourself on gathering information.

DON'T FORGET

Make sure you know both the limitations and benefits of the methods you used to gather information.

GATHERING INFORMATION ON THE PHYSICAL FACTOR – SKILL

OVERVIEW

Skills analysis can be carried out using observation schedules. Observation schedules are written tables that allow elements of performances to be recorded during or after a performance. Analysis can take place either during the performance for immediate feedback, or after the performance. They are often coupled with **video analysis** so the performer can complete their own analysis (after the performance using the recording). Alternatively, the performer can have another person (possibly their coach)

complete the observation schedule for them during the performance.

The schedules are easily adapted and when specific information is input, will allow for information to be gathered on physical, social, emotional and mental factors. In addition, the schedules will allow you to collect initial data to gain a broad overview of performance and also focused data to gain specific information. This will then enable you to plan future performance development.

ONLINE

Examples of observation schedules for match analysis can be found online at www.brightredbooks.net

MATCH SKILLS ANALYSIS

A **match skills analysis** is an example of an observation table that will allow you to analyse your skills within a match of your chosen activity. In the table you will list the skills of the activity down the left column. The other columns will measure your effectiveness in terms of your performance of the skills. To be deemed **effective** means you find success in producing the desired purpose and outcome of the skill. The level of effectiveness has to relate to the quality of the performance.

MOVEMENT SKILLS ANALYSIS

If you know the weaknesses in your performance, you can analyse them closer to identify the skills that are the main development needs, and you would then complete another more focussed observation schedule to identify the part of the skill that requires development. Focused data considers more **detailed** collection about your performance. This investigation takes the form of a movement or technical analysis which will give you help with the specific aspect of a weak skill that requires improvement.

The observation schedule is designed as a table and should be filled in by a knowledgeable observer. This analysis should take place in a **closed environment** where the performer is repeatedly executing the specific skill, such as a closed practice drill situation.

The movement skills analysis table will break the specific skill down into three phases:

- **preparation**
- **action**
- **recovery**.

DON'T FORGET

This type of movement analysis is used to observe a performance of a specific skill.

Under each phase will be a list of the movements or features of that particular part of the skill. These features are taken from the **model performance** of that skill. This table is then used to **compare** your performance against the features of the model performer.

Benefits of using observation schedules

- They can provide a broad overview of performance (all skills) and can also be adapted to provide more focused data, allowing you to look more closely at one skill.
- They are **valid** because they provide objective/statistical/factual data.
- They allow comparison to a model performer and/or the quality features of skills and techniques.
- Results are easy and quick to interpret, giving immediate feedback.
- They can identify **causes** of poor performance and identify an area of focus for training.
- They are a permanent record of performance, and can be used at a later date for comparative purposes.
- They are **reliable** sources of evidence as a knowledgeable observer completed it.

ONLINE

Examples of observation schedules for movement analysis can be found online at www.brightredbooks.net

LIMITATIONS OF USING OBSERVATION SCHEDULES

- It can be difficult for the observer to see every shot and record it.
- The observer's judgement is subjective and may not be accurate.
- Observer can lose concentration or be prejudiced by other factors.
- Environmental issues, such as the weather, can impact on the performance, depending on the activity.

Scattergraph

A scattergraph is another example of focused data. It is more visual and therefore results can be read easily at a glance.

Benefits of using scattergraphs

- Measures the effectiveness of each attempt by showing where the shuttle lands.
- Adaptable to any stroke. Valid as it only measures the accuracy / consistency of a stroke being investigated.
- Highlights if the performer can place the shuttle consistently in the designated area.
- The scattergraph can be used in conjunction with an observation schedule and video analysis to ensure it is accurate.

Limitations of using scattergraphs

- The crosses may not be the exact location of the shuttle.
- Can be time consuming to complete.
- Observer has to be concentrating for it to be accurate.

VIDEO ANALYSIS

Video analysis is widely used as it is an accurate record of your performance. Many devices can be used to record including video cameras, tablets and mobile phones. In addition, video recording will enable data to be gathered on every factor where the actions and behaviours can be viewed easily.

Benefits of using video analysis

- Can be used in conjunction with other methods of gathering information.
- Provides a visual demonstration to help identify a specific development need within a performance.
- For fast games, playback and slow motion will allow you to view performance repeatedly and ensure that you do not miss any skills or details.
- Looking at action more times makes it easier when identifying bad habits or patterns in technique.
- Allows performers to see for themselves what others are commenting on.
- Feedback can be provided immediately.
- Can focus on detail as this will allow you to observe movements more accurately.

Limitations of using video analysis

- Accessing equipment can be difficult.
- Technology can fail, run out of battery and data could be lost.
- The full process can be time consuming including the performance and watching of it.

THINGS TO DO AND THINK ABOUT

Analyse a method that you have used during your course to gather information on the physical skill factor. Consider the following:

- How reliable is it and why?
- What makes it a valid method?
- What limitations surround it?
- What are the benefits of using this method?

ONLINE

An example scattergraph is provided at www.brightredbooks.net showing a badminton court and overhead clears being played.

DON'T FORGET

If a question is worth 4 marks, you will need to state four separate bullet points and provide an example for each.

DON'T FORGET

Video analysis can be used to gather information on all four factors – physical, mental, emotional and social and will complement a variety of other methods of gathering information.

ONLINE TEST

Test yourself on gathering information at www.brightredbooks.net

GATHERING INFORMATION ON THE PHYSICAL FACTOR – TACTICS

In team games there are many different ways to gather information on the performance of individual players or teams as a whole.

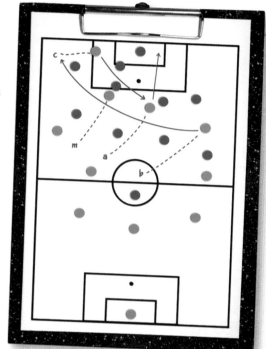

SCORE SHEETS

Some team match **score sheets** can tell you lots of useful information. With this information you can analyse what it means and use it to help you plan your tactics for following games such as:

- selecting the most appropriate players to start and take set plays

- identifying if fitness at the end of a game is an issue

- making decisions on substitutions, before players are fouled out

- deciding who to closely mark in opposing teams

- working on managing emotions if discipline record is having a negative impact on performance.

Benefits of using score sheets

- Gives you quantitative data that is objective and reliable.

- Identifies the scoring pattern of the game when points/goals were awarded.

- Tells you what players score points/goals, in own and opposing team.

- Informs you when a team lose points in the game (early, late or in middle).

- States how points/goals are scored, open play, penalties, corners, etc.

- Provides a discipline record of players, in own and opposing teams.

- Can inform tactics for future games.

- Helps you to make decisions regarding substitutions or starting teams.

Limitations of using score sheets

- Information does not tell you the story behind the game (poor weather, injury, etc).

- Does not highlight the work rate of all players.

- Does not provide any qualitative analysis.

DON'T FORGET

Score sheets are useful when gathering information on your competitive performance.

DON'T FORGET

Score sheets provide factual, quantitative data.

LEAGUE TABLES

League tables can tell you if teams are high or low scorers or concede lots of points or if they are a good defensive unit. It will also give you an overview of how they are playing that season as far as winning or losing games is concerned whilst **statistics** can help you find out high and low scorers in teams.

Benefits of using league tables

- Clearly identify individual or whole team areas of performance strength and weakness.
- Provides quantitative data to help you monitor and evaluate progress.
- Provides individual players with measurable data from within the game.
- Can assist players to identify development needs for their PDPs.
- Gives you benchmarks to be compared later on in the season.

Limitations of using league tables

- Does not identify how well a team perform tactics, the effort or application of performers.
- Information could be misleading.
- Does not provide any qualitative analysis.

SCOUTING REPORTS AND VIDEO FOOTAGE

Many professional teams will watch opponents prior to playing them. Gathering information in this way enables coaches to build a picture of how the opponents like to play and identify strengths and weaknesses. Similarly, watching yourself perform allows you to build this picture. With this information we can make an appropriate game plan or tactic to try and win the competition.

Benefits of using scouting reports and video footage

- Identify opponents strengths and weaknesses.
- Identify your own strengths and weaknesses.
- Provides quantitative data to help you monitor and evaluate progress.
- Provides individual players and teams with measurable data from within the game.
- Can assist players in identifying development needs for their PDPs.
- Gives benchmarks to be compared later on in the season.

Limitations of using scouting reports and video footage

- Only as good as the knowledge and experience of the person doing the observation and analysis.
- Information could be misleading.
- Does not provide any quantitative analysis.

THINGS TO DO AND THINK ABOUT

Analyse one method of electronic technology that you have used to gather information on your performance. Consider the following:
- How reliable is it and why?
- What makes it a valid method?
- What are the limitations?
- What are the benefits of using this method?

 **DON'T FORGET**

Video footage can be used in conjunction with other methods to allow you to complete observation schedules more accurately.

 **DON'T FORGET**

Observation schedules are easily adapted and can be used to gather information on tactical elements within an activity.

 VIDEO LINK

Watch the clip at www.brightredbooks.net to show how an iPad can help with video analysis, before, during and after a competitive football match.

 ONLINE TEST

Head to www.brightredbooks.net to test yourself on gathering information.

GATHERING INFORMATION ON THE MENTAL FACTOR

SPORT COMPETITION ANXIETY TEST

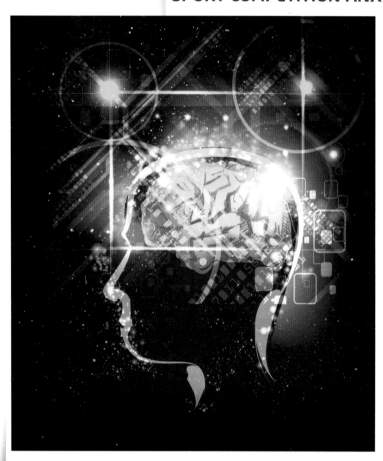

A **Sport Competition Anxiety Test** (SCAT) will give an insight into how a performer feels in a competitive situation by answering a series of statements . The results give some insight into levels of sporting anxiety.

Benefits of using a SCAT

- Quick and easy to complete, and can be accessed online and provides useful information.

- Reliable, due to the consistency of the questions.

- It is a recognised method. This increases the validity of results, and allows comparisons to be made against norms. Once results are calculated they can be compared against an average statistics table.

Limitations of using a SCAT

- The performer must be honest otherwise results are not valid or reliable

- The performer can only answer on the choices given. However, there may be other mental influences that affect their performance that are not considered in this test

ONLINE

Complete the online SCAT test at www.brightredbooks.net

ONLINE

Visit www.brightredbooks.net to see what this evaluation sheet looks like.

DON'T FORGET

Evaluations tend to be subjective in nature, therefore a knowledgeable other should conduct this.

PLAYER EVALUATION SHEET

A **player evaluation sheet** is used to measure decision-making abilities. A knowledgeable observer will watch you perform a full game of your chosen activity and will mark down how often you made particular decisions. The observer should also make a comment on this particular element of performance.

Benefits of using player evaluation sheets

- Can be useful when used in conjunction with video analysis to let you see the decisions you take while performing and why this may be the case.

- Easy to use and results are easy to interpret.

Limitations of player evaluation sheets

- Based on the observer's opinion.

- May not take account of game conditions, environment or situation which means it would be difficult to compare if the method was to be repeated.

- There is no guarantee that the selected decisions will occur.

MENTAL PERFORMANCE EVALUATION

A **mental performance evaluation** is another example of an observation table. The performer can have an observer complete the table during their performance, or complete it themselves after in conjunction with a recording. It can be adapted to evaluate a variety of mental sub-factors or by focussing on one in particular.

Benefits of using mental performance evaluation

- Experienced teacher or coach can give an accurate analysis of problems.

- Previous knowledge of performer allows quick analysis if it is a recurring problem. This gives an independent view of the decision-making process and makes feedback more valid.

- Coach can identify the strengths and weaknesses of an opponent and their game plan, and how it affects you.

Limitations of using mental performance evaluation

- If an observer is filling in the table it may be difficult to see all of the aspects listed making results less reliable.

- It can be difficult to make a judgement on the aspects listed until the full match has been played. This could make results less reliable.

 THINGS TO DO AND THINK ABOUT

What must you consider when completing an observation table in order to make it a valid and reliable source of gathering information? Consider:
- Who would complete it and why?
- How would it be filled in and why? (Under what conditions?)
- What information would you expect to gather?
- What would you do with the information that you gather?

 ONLINE

Visit www.brightredbooks.net to see an example of a mental performance evaluation for concentration.

DON'T FORGET

Various methods of gathering information can be adapted to suit your chosen factor.

ONLINE TEST

Test yourself on gathering information at www.brightredbooks.net

DON'T FORGET

Observation schedules can be used to gather information on many different factors and sub factors.

GATHERING INFORMATION ON THE EMOTIONAL AND SOCIAL FACTORS

METHODS OF COLLECTING INFORMATION ON THE EMOTIONAL FACTOR

Sports profile

A **sports profile** is a graphic profiler that rates your emotions in a wheel that visually represents your strengths and weaknesses. Within this collection of circles you place dots on the line that best describes your emotional stability within that factor. A model performer with exceptional emotional control will have a large perfectly round circle.

Benefits of using a sports profile

- Quick and easy to fill in.
- Provides qualitative information.
- This is a recognised test and therefore results can be compared against norms.
- Can provide benchmark data that can be compared later on.

Limitations of using a sports profile

- The performer needs to be honest and in tune with their emotions.
- Data is entirely subjective and could be misleading.
- The enormity of the competition will vary from performer to performer so may not allow for a comparison to be made.

Sports Emotions Questionnaire

This is where you complete a questionnaire regarding your emotional state prior to or after your performance. This will highlight the sub-factors you should focus on.

Benefits of using a sports emotions questionnaire

- Quick and easy to fill in.
- This is a recognised test and therefore results can be compared against norms.
- Can provide benchmark data that can be compared later on.

Limitations of using a sports emotions questionnaire

- The performer needs to be honest and in tune with own emotions.
- The enormity of the competition will vary from performer to performer so may not allow for a comparison to be made.

ONLINE

Visit wwww.brightredbooks.net to see an example of a profiler.

ONLINE

Visit www.brightredbooks.net to see an example of a sports emotion questionnaire.

DON'T FORGET

Gathering information can occur at the beginning, middle and end of your competitive season to ensure a more informed comparison.

METHODS OF COLLECTING INFORMATION ON THE SOCIAL FACTOR

Most of the methods that are used to gather information on the social factors tend to involve qualitative analysis (opinion, not fact). The methods normally consider the opinion and reflection of the performer themselves and observers such as a class mate, teacher or a coach.

contd

Questionnaires

A questionnaire is a good way of identifying social factors because the questions can be made specific to any given situation and also to different aspects within the social factor.

Benefits of using questionnaires

- Quick and easy to fill in.
- This is a recognised test and therefore results can be compared against norms.
- Can provide benchmark data that can be compared later on.

Limitations of using questionnaires

- The performer needs to be honest and in tune with own emotions.
- The enormity of the competition will vary from performer to performer so may not allow for a comparison to be made.

Feedback from coach and verbal feedback from players

Coaches can give players any relevant information they feel necessary either before, during or after a performance. This may take the form of individual or group meetings, team talks, time outs, half time and post-match analysis.

Players can give feedback to coaches on the way an individual player or team is playing at any point in a match.

Benefits of using coach feedback

- Coaches are knowledgeable and give great insight.
- Feedback can be given almost instantaneously.
- Coaches can choose to give feedback on the most important development need.
- Players feel like they have a voice and are empowered to improve.
- Can assist players to identify development needs for their PDPs.

Limitations of using coach feedback

- Performers may not agree with the feedback.
- Information can be subjective and based on negative feelings.
- Does not provide any quantitative analysis.
- Players' feedback can be subjective, misleading and not representative of all players.

> **DON'T FORGET**
>
> Many benefits and limitations are transferable across different methods.

 THINGS TO DO AND THINK ABOUT

Devise a questionnaire for a factor of your choice. Consider the following:
- What factor are you trying to gain information about?
- What types of questions will provide you with the information that you are looking for?

 ONLINE TEST

Test yourself on gathering information at www.brightredbooks.net

MODEL PERFORMERS

As we look at various methods of gathering information it is important to consider the important role that **model performers** can have in helping us gather information. Skilled performers are often referred to as model performers. Top class sports people would be considered models that we can aspire to. They are athletes performing at an elite level in their field.

SKILLED PERFORMANCE

The skilled performance has certain qualities that are common to all types of activities. The skilled performance displays:

- linked movements carried out with maximum efficiency
- a high quality of movement is produced consistently throughout the performance
- sequences of movements that show control and fluency with minimum effort
- selection of the correct options for effective performance
- effective use of time within the performance
- economic use of movement, creativity, flair, deception.

Using a model performance – Benefits

Considering a model performance can help us in many ways:

- Shows an example of high quality performance (few errors, good decision-making under pressure, etc).
- Gives a good source of motivation and inspiration. This will give us a clear goal to work towards. It will also help us to set appropriate targets and goals.
- Gives a clear picture of high level performance.
- Acts as a standard to compare with our own performance. This allows us to identify our performance strengths and weaknesses. After identifying areas of weakness in our performance we have evidence to create appropriate development plans to address any issues.
- Provides evidence to help us to devise appropriate starting point for development programmes.
- Provides baseline data to compare against at a later date. This will help us to monitor and evaluate our development programme.

In order to aspire to a model performance we must first gather information on our current performance level and compare them against each other. After this comparison is made a plan of action can be devised to improve upon our current standard of play.

APPROPRIATENESS OF COLLECTION METHODS

The method that you select to collect information on your performance has to be appropriate. Basically this means that it needs to be right and practical for your individual performance requirements. The activity we participate in, our stage of learning, the factor(s) we are gathering information on and the practicalities, will all contribute to the appropriateness of the method.

contd

ONLINE

Watch the clip at www.brightredbooks.net to see examples of model performers.

DON'T FORGET

There are both benefits and limitations to using a model performer. Some limitations are performers becoming demotivated, poor comparisons being made and the lack of understanding around variations in successful techniques.

DON'T FORGET

In the exam you will need to be able to justify why you selected your method of gathering information.

In order to ensure that your method is appropriate you should consider the following:

- the validity and reliability of methods
- the specificity of methods to the factor
- the ease of carrying out methods
- the consideration of specialist equipment/cost implications
- the protocols of the method
- any other relevant considerations.

INTERPRETATION OF QUALITATIVE/ QUANTITATIVE, OBJECTIVE/SUBJECTIVE DATA

The methods of collecting information are a mixture of quantitative and qualitative information, and subjective and objective data.

OBJECTIVE
Factual
Direct Observations
Countable
Reproductive
Unbiased

"Expertise"
There's a lot of
good stuff in here!

SUBJECTIVE
Opinion
Judgement
Preference
Belief
Rumour
Suspicion

Qualitative data

Qualitative data tends to be **opinion** based evidence and therefore can be subjective. This can be the opinion of the performer (internal) or another person such as a coach or team-mate (external). Methods such as questionnaires, team meetings, training diaries, coach feedback and internal feedback are obvious examples of qualitative data. Qualitative data is often used to measure performance on an ongoing, continuous basis.

Quantitative data

Quantitative data tends to be **statistically** based and therefore is more objective. Methods such as observation schedules, match and movement analysis tables and standardised fitness tests all provide a 'score' or statistic which we can use. Performers are **judged against a set criteria** and their level of success is recorded. Quantitative data can be easy to collate and see results but can sometimes be problematic to collect due to resources such as people and specialist equipment.

IDENTIFICATION OF STRENGTHS AND AREAS FOR DEVELOPMENT

With the information we collect on our performance we need to **analyse** the results and come to a conclusion about our strengths and development needs. To analyse this information it may help to place it on various graphic organisers (graphs, profilers, tables, etc), as this will help you to examine the data and identify where your strengths lie. The opportunity to see for yourself through video analysis is also important, especially if the data contradicts your personal thoughts and feelings.

 THINGS TO DO AND THINK ABOUT

Describe the qualities a model performer displays in an activity of your choice.

DEVELOPING PERFORMANCE CONSIDERATIONS

PERFORMANCE DEVELOPMENT PLANNING

PURPOSE OF PERFORMANCE DEVELOPMENT PLANNING

Effective performance development planning is needed in order to ensure that we reach our goals and are successful during our performance. Improvements will be incremental over time if planning involves strategically setting SMART targets:

- **s**pecific
- **m**anageable
- **a**chievable
- **r**ealistic
- **t**ime-phased.

Programmes of work need to be carefully prepared to meet the demands of your activity and get you ready for competition. What you do will be unique to yourself, your own fitness levels, stage of learning and prior experience, so thorough analysis of your fitness is needed before you can plan an appropriate development programme. The purpose and value of performance development planning is to:

- break down your performance goals into SMART targets
- take account all relevant principles of training or practice
- avoid a performance plateau
- keep you motivated and confident
- ensure your programme is specific to your individual needs
- limit boredom when training
- ensure that you do not overtrain and burn out
- concentrate on the most important aspect, eliminating unproductive efforts
- provide a sense of direction
- allow you to achieve your performance goals.

When preparing for different competitions, matches or meets the aims and objectives may be different. We need to plan for the unique performance by considering a number of factors. The following factors will be considered:

- cycle of analysis
- skill classification
- phase of training (periodisation)
- stage of learning
- principles of effective practice
- principles of training
- training methods (physical, mental, emotional and social).

DON'T FORGET

SMART targets will enable incremental progress whilst maintaining your motivation.

DON'T FORGET

Your development need tends to be the weakest part of your performance.

ONLINE

A full breakdown of all the sub-factors can be found at www.brightredbook.net

PRIORITISING DEVELOPMENT NEEDS

It is vitally important that we prioritise when planning for improvement as this allows us to set SMART targets. To prioritise you have to analyse the mental, emotional, social and physical factors that currently impact on your performance. You can do this by examining the information you have gathered from both within and outwith competitions. Then you evaluate your performance to identify aspects that need some development. If you identified no aspects, that is notably weaker. For each aspect that needs development, you will need to prioritise what you will work on during training, so that you improve and are ready for competition. There are a number of things you need to consider when prioritising your development needs:

- weakest aspect of your performance
- data from general observations that provides evidence of this weakness
- tactics and strategies requiring you to learn or develop your performance
- how long you have before your performance
- your opponents strengths and weaknesses
- the weather, facilities and training resources
- criteria of successful performance
- short, medium and long-term goals.

CYCLE OF ANALYSIS

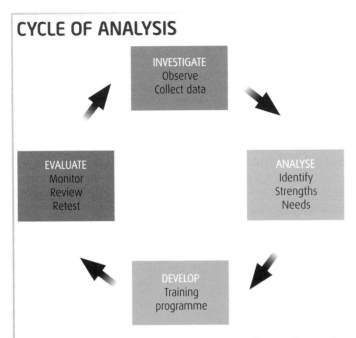

The cycle of analysis is an approach that can be used to analyse and improve performance. It involves four key stages:

- investigation
- analysis
- development
- evaluation.

In your Higher Physical Education course you will work through the cycle for all of your activities in order to improve your practical performance. The objective of the cycle is to ensure that there is continual improvement and no plateau in your learning. The cycle could continue throughout a training season or over a number of years. The cycle represents the need for you to come back to the starting point in order to re-evaluate your whole performance once more and identify new development needs. Even elite performers follow this cycle as competitors at the top of their game are never satisfied and always striving to improve.

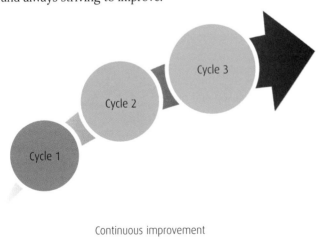

Continuous improvement

DON'T FORGET

There are four key stages to the cycle of analysis and monitoring should occur at each stage.

DON'T FORGET

The cycle of analysis is a development approach that you will use continually throughout your performance career. It helps you to progress and avoid a plateau in your performance.

THINGS TO DO AND THINK ABOUT

1 State the four stages of the cycle of analysis.

2 Explain what happens during each stage of the cycle.

3 Outline a number of reasons why adopting this approach to improve performance would be beneficial.

ONLINE TEST

Complete the online test at www.brightredbooks.net on the cycle of analysis.

SKILL CLASSIFICATIONS

SKILLED PERFORMANCE

A skilled performer makes it look easy! They have a variety of shots at their disposal and they play the appropriate shot at the appropriate time – **good decision-making skills**. Their movement is **economical, fluent** and **controlled**. Their shots are **accurate** and show the correct amount of touch. They **position themselves correctly, anticipate accurately** and **react quickly**. Skilled performers provide a good model for the types of performances to aspire to. A model performance can be many things, but primarily it is the skilled performance that we hope to achieve, and work towards.

CATEGORIES OF SKILLS

There are three different categories for classifying skills:
- closed/open
- simple/complex
- discrete/serial/continuous.

Closed/open skills

Closed ←————————————————————————→ Open

A **closed** skill is internally paced and performed in the same way every time you play. An example is a short or high serve in badminton. There are no external variables that can affect the performance of the skill.

Very little affects the way you do this skill because circumstances are the same every time you play it – the court is the same size, it is indoor so it is not affected by the weather, and so on. You decide where you are going to stand to play it and where you are putting the shuttle.

An **open** skill is performed differently every time you play it because of the circumstances surrounding the skill, such as the weather and ground conditions, the height, speed and direction of the ball, and the presence of competing players.

 **ACTIVITY**

For each sport shown in the table, identify closed and open skills which would feature in a competitive event.

ACTIVITY	CLOSED SKILL	OPEN SKILL
Basketball		
Gymnastics		
Hockey		
Dance		
Tennis		

Simple/complex skills

Simple ←————————————————————————→ Complex

Simple skills have few parts and are easy to learn and perform, such as a tennis serve. The player has both racket and ball in hand when performing the serve. They are stationary and do not have to react to a moving ball.

contd

Complex skills have sub-routines and are more difficult to co-ordinate, making them more difficult to learn and to perform. The spike is an example of a complex skill in volleyball.

The player has to react to the height and direction of the set in order to time their run up and jump to contact the ball at its highest height.

 **ACTIVITY**

For each sport shown in the table, identify simple and complex skills which would feature in a competitive event.

ACTIVITY	SIMPLE SKILL	COMPLEX SKILL
Football		
Netball		
Trampolining		
Rugby		
Athletics		

Discrete/serial and continuous skills

Discrete ←——————————→ Serial ←——————————→ Continuous

Discrete skills have a beginning and an end, such as the long jump.

Serial skills are usually complex because they are made up of different parts which have to be put together to complete the skill. In badminton we could use the smash as an example – the player moves to get behind the incoming shuttle, transfers weight to perform the smash then recovers balance and moves to the ready position for the return.

Continuous skills are repeated constantly. Cyclists and rowers constantly repeat the same action to perform their activity.

 THINGS TO DO AND THINK ABOUT

Choose activities and identify the appropriate type of skill to complete the table below.

ACTIVITY	DISCRETE SKILL	SERIAL SKILL	CONTINUOUS SKILL

PHASES OF TRAINING

WHY USE PHASES OF TRAINING?

Preparation Phase	→	Competition Phase	→	Transition Phase

DON'T FORGET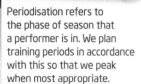

Periodisation refers to the phase of season that a performer is in. We plan training periods in accordance with this so that we peak when most appropriate.

A training plan is usually blocked into periods of time, to give **phases of training**, otherwise known as **periodisation**. The time periods can be weeks, months or years, dependent on the performance goals. During the different phases or periods of training, activity intensity and volume alters to prepare the performer adequately for the challenges ahead.

A training or development plan should recognise the fact that no athlete can maintain peak performance all year round, so the plan is strategically created to allow for a number of smaller peaks in performance throughout the year. These peaks would be planned to occur before trials, important games, events and competitions, and generally at the end of a season or performance year. A phased training plan also avoids burn out and should stop athletes becoming disillusioned, which is a particular problem if performance appears to get stuck at a plateau.

CYCLES OF TRAINING

Periodic training systems typically divide time up into three types of cycles:

- **Microcycle** - training plan that takes place over a week.

- **Mesocycle** - training plan anywhere from two weeks to a few months (but typically six weeks)

- **Macrocycle** - overall training period, usually representing a year. There are three phases of the macrocycle:
  - **preparation**   - **competition**   - **transition**

A typical macrocycle phase includes the following elements:

- **Preparation** General preparation and specific preparation. The objective is to attain previous training state.

- **Competition** The phase containing competitions or events each contains a pre-competitive and a main competition phase. Within the main competition phase, an uploading phase and a special preparatory phase may be included

- **Recovery** This phase facilitates psychological rest and biological regeneration, whilst maintaining an acceptable level of general physical fitness. This phase should not exceed five weeks under normal conditions and may be sports specific.

DON'T FORGET

Elite professional athletes have longer phases, which usually work round the periods of major sporting events such as World Championships and Olympic Games.

A development programme comprises microcycles, or **weekly plans**, that are part of a mesocycle, or **training block**. A number of mesocycles will lead up to the competition phase. These mesocycles alter in intensity to ensure that performance peaks when required. A final mesocycle will make up the transition phase and complete the macrocycle.

MACROCYCLE																												
Preparation						Competition																		Recovery				
Mesocycle 1						Mesocycle 2						Mesocycle 3						Mesocycle 4						Mesocycle 5				
Week						Week						Week						Week						Week				
1	2	3	4	5	6	1	2	3	4	5	6	1	2	3	4	5	6	1	2	3	4	5	6	1	2	3	4	5

contd

The example shown here shows a six week mesocycle.

BLOCK PLAN (6 weeks mesocycle)						
	Week 1	Week 2	Week 3	Week 4	Week 5	Week 6
Monday	Continuous run 20 minute	Continuous run 25 minute	Continuous run 30 minute	Fartlek 30 minutes 75% jog 25% sprint	Fartlek 30 minutes 75% jog 25% sprint	Fartlek 30 minutes 75% jog 25% sprint
Tuesday	Skills session 4x15 minutes	Skills session 4x17 minutes	Skills session 3x20 minutes	Skills session 3x22 minutes	Skills session 2x30 minutes	Skills session 2x35 minutes
Wednesday	Rest day	Rest day	Rest day	Rest day	Rest day	Rest day
Thursday	Fartlek 20 minutes 75% jog 25% sprint	Fartlek 25 minutes 75% jog 25% sprint	Fartlek 25 minutes 75% jog 25% sprint	Fartlek 30 minutes 75% jog 25% sprint	Fartlek 30 minutes 75% jog 25% sprint	Fartlek 30 minutes 75% jog 25% sprint
Friday	Rest day	Rest day	Rest day	Rest day	Rest day	Rest day
Saturday	Game	Game	Game	Game	Game	Game
Sunday	20 minute recovery run and stretch	22 minute recovery run and stretch	25 minute recovery run and stretch	27 minute recovery run and stretch	30 minute recovery run and stretch	32 minute recovery run and stretch

 ## THINGS TO DO AND THINK ABOUT

Look at the two different examples of sessions extracted from a PDP.

What are your observations? Consider some of the following **principles of training** to help you evaluate:

- Specificity
- Progression
- Overload
- Reversibility
- Tedium
- You can also comment on any other aspects that you feel are relevant.

Example

Aim – to improve CRE/Decision making – Volleyball

Baseline/initial data – 20m progressive shuttle run test score of 5.5, decision making questionnaire showing decisions were made too slowly

	Note your observations here:	What impact do you think this would have on the performer? Put yourself in their shoes.
Session 1 –Monday Warm up – 20 minute jog at 80% MHR. Treadmill running – 20 minutes running – continuous training at 80% MHR Cool down – 10 minutes – jog and stretch Decision making theory based lesson – 1 hour in class		
Session 2 – Tuesday Warm up – 25 minute jog at 80% MHR 25 minute interval training on volley ball court Decision making drills – who to set to – 30 minutes Cool down – 10 minutes – jog and stretch		
After 1 week of training CRE was re-tested using 12 minute Cooper test	**Evaluate their chosen monitoring process ...**	

1 Identify where the programme would fit into in the annual plan.

2 Provide reasons for your answer.

 **DON'T FORGET**

The cycles of training chunk training down into smaller time frames. Within each training cycles, different targets and goals are set. The targets must be meaningful, achievable and time-phased.

 ONLINE TEST

Test yourself on the phases of training online at www.brightredbooks.net

STAGES OF LEARNING

OVERVIEW

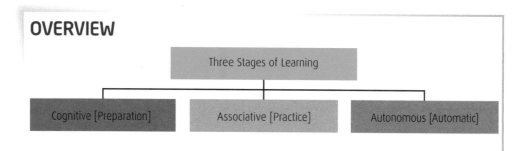

Three Stages of Learning

Cognitive [Preparation] | Associative [Practice] | Autonomous [Automatic]

DON'T FORGET

Your stage of learning directly impacts on the types of practices you should use. Consider this when planning your Personal Development Plan (PDP).

Learning anything new can be broken down into stages, as we move from the initial stages when we are unfamiliar with the skill or technique through to being fully proficient. We need to consider the stage of learning that we are in at any particular time so that we can plan the most appropriate programme to meet our needs. With this knowledge we will be able to apply how best to prepare to develop our performance and progress.

The three stages of learning are:

- **cognitive**
- **associative**
- **autonomous**

and are described more fully in the table.

CHARACTERISTICS		
Cognitive (preparation)	**Associative** (practice)	**Autonomous** (automatic)
Lacks movement and fluency	Some fluency of movement and accuracy	Movement is fluid
Technique is poor, inaccurate	Technique is inconsistent	Technique is accurate
Lacks confidence	Some confidence	Extremely confident
Lots of unforced errors	Becoming more consistent	Consistent with little errors
No attempt at disguise	Beginning to attempt disguise	Disguise in lots of skills
Decision making is poor	Decision-making is inconsistent	Correct decisions made often
LEARNERS NEED		
Cognitive (preparation)	**Associative** (practice)	**Autonomous** (automatic)
Demonstrations and verbal explanations	Demonstrations especially of model performers	Focus on tactical constraints (as skills are automatic so they have more time)
Opportunity to shadow	Assistance to set own aims and objectives	Less feedback and opportunity to be self corrective
Set aims and objectives	Varied practices increasing the pressure	To work with others on team objectives
Short, simple practices	Some external feedback	
Focus on technical efficiency	Opportunity for intrinsic feedback	
Quality external feedback	Repetitive practices	
Frequent rest and lots of time		

VIDEO LINK

Watch the clip of a performer at the practice stage at www.brightredbooks.net

SUITABLE PRACTICE METHODS		
Cognitive (preparation)	**Associative** (practice)	**Autonomous** (automatic)
Shadow practices	Repetition drills	Complex drills
Passive practices	More active practices	Pressure practices
Repetition drills	Whole-part-whole	Active practices
Gradual build-up	Gradual build-up	Combination drills
	Combination drills	Conditioned games
	Conditioned games	

 **ACTIVITY**

Suggest reasons why the performers in the video are at the practice stage. Make sure you justify your answer.

 **ACTIVITY**

Now look at two other clips and identify what stage of learning the performer is at. Provide reasons for your answers and check your answers at www.brightredbooks.net.

 THINGS TO DO AND THINK ABOUT

1   Think of a skill or activity or sport that you have never tried before. What stage of learning will you be at?

2   How do you think you will feel when trying this for the first time?

3   List the features that would help you to learn. What would you need to hear, see and feel?

4   What do you think you would look like to onlookers? What characteristics would you display to a coach or peer?

5   Take yourself through the stages of learning with a simple activity.

   (a) Experience being at the cognitive stage of learning. Try to play an activity with your weak hand or foot, or try writing with your weak hand.

   (b) Experience being at the practice stage by repeating the action over and over again until you gradually get better or more fluent at it.

   (c) Experience being at the autonomous stage by swapping back to your good hand or foot and feeling how easy it now seems.

6   Complete the table to outline the characteristics of performers at each stage of learning in your chosen activity.

Activity of choosing:		
STAGE OF LEARNING	CHARACTERISTICS	LEARNERS NEED
Cognitive (preparation)		
Associative (practice)		
Autonomous (automatic)		

7   Discuss with a friend, teacher family member how it would feel to be at each stage.

8   Explain what you would take into consideration when planning a development programme for a learner at each stage.

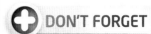 **DON'T FORGET**

Link your answer to the characteristics for this stage of learning.

 **DON'T FORGET**

As learners progress through the stages of learning they will begin to need less **external** feedback as they rely more on their **internal** selves.

 **VIDEO LINK**

Watch the clip at www.brightredbooks.net and justify what makes Colin Jackson an automatic model performer in his field.

 **DON'T FORGET**

You must be able to **justify** a learners' stage of learning by linking their skill level to the characteristics. You must also be able to **explain** the link between skill classification and the types of practices and approaches that you would employ to improve them.

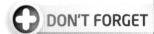 **ONLINE TEST**

Complete the online test at www.brightredbooks.net

 **DON'T FORGET**

Justify a learner's stage of learning by linking their skill level to the characteristics.

 **DON'T FORGET**

Explain the link between stage of learning and the types of practices and approaches that you would use to improve them.

PRINCIPLES OF TRAINING AND EFFECTIVE PRACTICE

PRINCIPLES OF TRAINING

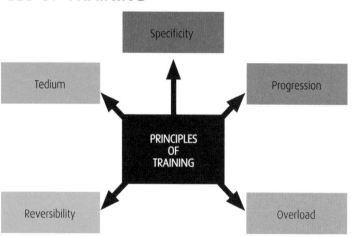

DON'T FORGET

Use the acronym **SPORT** to help you remember the principles of training.

DON'T FORGET

The principles of training generally refer to training sessions and plans involving the development of physical fitness.

When training it is vital that you follow a set of principles to ensure you continually develop and progress. The principles are a set of rules that provide guidance when constructing these training sessions, weekly plans (microcycle) block plans, (mesocycle) and yearly programmes (macrocycle).

Specificity

Specificity is the quality or condition of being appropriate to a performers individual needs. To be specific to these needs you would need to consider a performers chosen activity, stage of learning, the factor being developed and the appropriateness of training approach.

Progression

Progression is the process of developing gradually towards an advanced state. It can relate to passing through a series of stages such as the stages of learning, moving onto more progressive practices in the progression continuum and building up your mental, emotional, social and physical capabilities.

Overload

Overload describes a gradual increase in frequency (how often), intensity (how hard), duration (how long) and activity (how sport specific), in order to achieve the targeted goal of the performer. When your capacity is gently stretched you are overloaded and progressively developed and moved forward. Overload is essential to ensuring you continue to improve and do not plateau.

Reversibility

ONLINE

Head to www.brightredbooks.net for some activities on the principles of training and effective practice.

Reversibility means any adaptation that takes place as a result of training will be reversed when if you stop training, take a break, are injured or do not train often enough. You will lose fitness and begin to revert back to pre-training state. However it is also essential that adequate rest and recovery is build into programmes, to allow your body to recover. Well-planned days off after competition and not consecutively ensure that reversibility will not occur.

Tedium

Tedium relates to activities becoming boring or monotonous. Programmes have to have variety, be motivating and interesting to avoid tedium. This can be achieved with a competitive challenge throughout, making it activity and role specific, and doing practices for an appropriate period of time.

PRINCIPLES OF EFFECTIVE PRACTICE

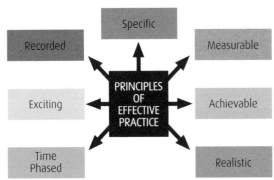

When planning sessions to develop skills and techniques the principles of effective practice provide some guidance aspects to consider. Following these rules will ensure that training sessions are both enjoyable and worthwhile.

PRINCIPLES OF EFFECTIVE PRACTICE	
Specific	Practices must be relevant to the performers ability and their experience. Needs to be sufficiently challenging, not too easy or hard. You need specific data analysis for factors or skills being observed. Training methods to the factor being trained and the method of training has to be appropriate for your stage of learning
Measurable	Quantitative or qualitative data that can measure your success. This helps you to set targets for improvement and keep track of your progress.
Achievable	Practices are designed so that you experience success and remain motivated. The progressive level of challenge should be very gradual and appropriate for your starting skill or fitness level. When you continually reach your target you will be motivated to progress onto new more difficult challenges.
Realistic	Practices should replicate a competitive situation. This will then make it easier for you to transfer it into your performance at the appropriate time. Gradual increase in the game demands and pressures will keep training realistic.
Time-Phased	Adequate time is allowed for you to improve your skills, factor or fitness, in your development plan. Training needs to take into account regular practice to ensure skills are not forgotten, rest periods to avoid fatigue, duration of practices to avoid boredom and intervals to maintain the quality and increase motivation.
Exciting	Practices should be exciting, challenging and fun. Short, fun and intensive training sessions are more beneficial than long dull sessions, as tedium and disinterest occurs and impacts on your concentration levels. Exciting sessions improve concentration and ensure intrinsic motivation is high.
Recordable	All practice results, goals, targets, thoughts and feelings are written down in your training diary. Recording your practice outcomes allows you to monitor this measurable data and check your progress. This will then allow you to set appropriate targets and goals and remain motivated and focussed on your overall goals.

 THINGS TO DO AND THINK ABOUT

1 Read your notes and then make your own notes to explain what is meant by the acronym SPORT.

2 Without looking at these notes explain to a classmate, family member, friend or teacher what is meant by SPORT.

3 In relation to your chosen activity explain how you planned a training programme that considers these principles.

4 Make your own notes to explain what is meant by the acronym SMARTER.

5 Without looking at these notes explain to a classmate, family member, friend or teacher what is meant by SMARTER.

6 Explain how you planned a training programme for your chosen activity that uses these principles.

APPROACHES TO DEVELOPING PERFORMANCE

TRAINING METHODS – PHYSICAL FITNESS

There are a number of different approaches that are required to meet physical development goals.

PHYSICAL		
Fitness	**Skills**	**Tactics**
Continuous training Fartlek training Interval training Circuit training	Shadow drills Repetitive practices Combination drills Opposed/unopposed Conditioned games	Modification or adaption of tactics or formations Rehearsal and walkthroughs Passive/active defender
MENTAL	**EMOTIONAL**	**SOCIAL**
Relaxation Visualisation Positive self-talk	Team talks Conflict management techniques Assertiveness training	Team building Restorative Partner group work

DON'T FORGET

There are other development approaches that you may have covered in your course.

DON'T FORGET

Your training zone is 70-85% of your maximum heart rate.

DON'T FORGET

Any exercise which allows you to work at differing intensities can be used.

ONLINE

Look at the examples of fartlek training at www.brightredbooks.net

CONTINUOUS TRAINING

This is physical action that occurs repeatedly for a prolonged period of time. It can take place in various forms, such as running, cycling or swimming, where you move continually to develop your aerobic endurance. The training principle of specificity should be considered when deciding on which form of training you will use.

The purpose of continuous training is to maintain a steady level of effort throughout the duration of training. Your heart rate must be in the correct training zone during training in order to make improvements to fitness. Training must also be progressively overloaded by increasing the intensity (how hard you train), frequency (how often you train) or duration (how long you train for,) to ensure your fitness continues to improve.

FARTLEK TRAINING

Fartlek training is defined as continuous movement with periods of fast movement intermixed with periods of slower movement. The word fartlek is Swedish for **speed play**. Fartlek training involves continuously working for a period of time where the intensity varies. This training should replicate the movement required in a particular activity. There could also be a change in terrain to increase or decrease intensity.

A typical fartlek session could include sprinting, running, jogging and walking with variations in direction of movement to fit in with the demands of their sport. It could be made more sport specific by including the control of an object (football, stick, racket etc) used in the sport.

INTERVAL TRAINING

Interval training is physical training consisting of alternating periods of high and low intensity activity. For example performers work for a set time or distance and then rest and recover for a set time or distance. Interval training can be applied to a variety of physical actions such as running, swimming, cycling or rowing. Interval training can be progressively overloaded by increasing the distance or time and decreasing the rest. It can be adapted to improve your CRE, speed or speed endurance by altering the work-to-rest ratio.

An example of an interval training session is shown in the table.

RATIO	DISTANCE	TIME	RECOVERY	FITNESS
1:3	20m	6 secs	18 secs	Speed
1:2	40m	12 secs	24 secs	Speed endurance
1:1	400m	60 secs	60 secs	CRE

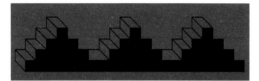

CIRCUIT TRAINING

Circuit training is a form of body conditioning or resistance training using high intensity aerobics. It involves completing a series of exercises or activities in a special order, working on different muscle groups. Exercises can be completed for a set number of repetitions or a set time before performers move on. For example, a circuit could be performed for 30 seconds at 100% effort with a 30 second rest. Circuits can be made up with exercises that are specific to different activities.

General Benefits of all Training Methods

- Proven to train your specific and identified development need
- Focusses on the aspect identified by your data analysis
- Most are relatively easy to set up on the appropriate playing surface.
- Can be progressively overloaded by increasing frequency, intensity and duration
- Most can be made more game specific by utilising activity specific exercises
- Can be adapted to suit skill or fitness levels
- Will positively impact on your general development

General Limitations of all Training Methods

- Will never exactly replicate the game or performance situation
- Could be boring or not appropriate if poorly planned
- Usually only trains individual factors or skills at the one time so other aspects of performance may suffer
- Knowledge and understanding is required to ensure performers know the purpose of approach/method
- If not individually adapted they can have little impact
- Does not truly require the same decision making and problem solving used in competitive situations
- Performers require an open mind to try something new that they may have no experience of

 **DON'T FORGET**

Circuit training targets strength building and muscular endurance, but it can also improve your CRE and power.

 **DON'T FORGET**

The principles of training must be applied to gain continued improvements in your fitness levels.

 ONLINE

Visit the following link to examine the rules of creating circuits.

 ONLINE TEST

Complete the test at www.brightredbooks.net on training.

 ## THINGS TO DO AND THINK ABOUT

1. Describe a continuous training you have taken part in.
   (a) Explain in detail what you did, where you did it, when you did it and how you prepared the session.
   (b) Explain the benefits of this type of training in relation to your chosen activity and the type of fitness required for you to perform successfully
   (c) State why you used this method of training, referring to your chosen activity.

2. Repeat Q1 describing a fartlek training you have taken part in (draw a diagram to help).

TRAINING METHODS – PHYSICAL SKILLS

SHADOW PRACTICE

Shadow practice is a method of learning a skill by mimicking the action without the ball or object. It usually occurs at the cognitive stage of learning but can be used at any time. It involves the performer working under no pressure to perform the required skill by mirroring the movement, footwork and correct preparation, action and recovery for the skill or technique.

During this stage it is vital to:
- **visualise the skill** through demonstrations of a model performance or viewing video footage to build up a mental picture of the skill
- **break the skill down** into a series of subroutines, using practices which involve only part of the skill or technique. This makes it easier to learn the skill or technique.

Practice sessions should be short in duration to avoid boredom but long enough for meaningful progress.

Benefits of shadow practice

- Easy to set up and no equipment required.
- Movements can be refined in all stages of action.
- Performers can progress from one stage of learning to the next.
- Actions become automatic and **muscle memory** is developed without any pressure.
- Practice can be progressed by increasing the number of subroutines of the action being mimicked.
- Focuses on the correct technique, movement and foot patterns.

REPETITION DRILLS

Repetition drills involves performing a skill in the same situation repeatedly. During a practice, at any stage of learning, it is vital that the movement is repeated over and over again. By doing this, muscles and nerves learn to move automatically in the newly learned way. You develop muscle memory and the skill becomes more natural, automatic and can be performed subconsciously.

Repetition drills can also be used to focus on and practice certain parts (subroutines) of a skill that require development. This lets you eliminate the distraction of the game and other skills as you develop the correct technique.

When completing repetition drills, it is important to vary the practice conditions and include appropriate rest periods to avoid boredom and fatigue.

Benefits of repetition drills

- They can be altered to take into account previous experience or stage of learning.
- Help skills to become automatic.
- Can be progressively overloaded by increasing reps or decreasing rest.
- Appropriate method of training for learners in the cognitive or intermediate stage of learning.
- Performers can practice individually or in pairs without a coach or team-mates.

COMBINATION DRILLS

Combination practices or drills involve linking skills and techniques to create a successful sequence of movements. In many activities combinations of skills are required to outmanoeuvre your opponents and set up winning opportunities. Combination drills can be used to link skills together to play certain tactics or strategies, and can work when both repetition and different degrees of pressure are involved.

Benefits of combination drills

- Performers can practice combinations of skills and techniques to fulfil the tactics.
- Can be progressively overloaded by making sequence of skills and techniques longer or more intricate.
- Can be used during the associative practice stage of learning leading towards the automatic stage.
- Develops skills in more competitive situations.
- Improves development of footwork and movement to link skills and techniques together.
- Skills requiring practice can be developed alongside other skills.

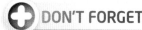

DON'T FORGET

In racket sports, combinations of shots ensure you move your opponent about the court and create space that you can exploit. In fighting sports, attacking and defending skills are combined to create opportunities for successful hits.

CONDITIONED GAMES

Conditioned games are bridging activities between practice and the game. They take the theme of the practice session and ensure that skills are practiced in context so that performers use the skills under the pressure of a real game. This helps develop decision-making and problem-solving in game-like scenarios.

In conditioned games the normal rules can be changed or altered to ensure that the appropriate skills, techniques or tactics are practiced more often. Other elements of the game can also be altered, such as the scoring system, playing areas, and size or height of scoring area.

Benefits of conditioned games

- Fun, enjoyable and meaningful.
- Skills, techniques or tactics are practiced in the context of a game.
- Helps develop decision-making and problem-solving.
- Can be progressed by decreasing the conditions and gently enabling more decision-making.
- Appropriate for performers at all stages of learning, by varying the conditions.

DON'T FORGET

Conditioned games can also be used to develop your chosen tactics and strategies in a game situation.

THINGS TO DO AND THINK ABOUT

1 Describe a shadow training drill you have taken part in.
   (a) Explain in detail what you did, where you did it, when you did it and how you prepared the session.
   (b) Explain the benefits of this type of training in relation to your chosen activity and the type of drills required for you to perform successfully.
   (c) State why you used this method of training, referring to your chosen activity.

2 Repeat Q1, describing a repetition drill, combination drill and a conditioned game that you have taken part in.

3 Consider and list the limitations of each training method.

ONLINE TEST

Complete the test at www.brightredbooks.net on shadow, repetition and combination drills and conditioned games.

TRAINING METHODS – PHYSICAL TACTICS

MODIFICATION OR ADAPTING STRATEGIES AND FORMATIONS

Modifying and adapting strategies or formations is a useful development approach as it allows performers to prepare for different scenarios and practice their decision-making. A coach or player will make tactical decisions before and during a performance which will affect the overall outcome of the performance. Adapting strategies can be developed in training by using conditioned games and setting up unique scenarios which may unfold during a game. This lets performers practice problem-solving and decision-making skills under pressure. It is important for a team or player to have several back-up plans that can be adapted to meet a changing scenario in competition.

Benefits of training for modification or adapting strategies and formations

- Lets players practice decision-making and problem solving in game scenarios.

- Prepares performers for the demands of competitions.

- Realistic, fun and enjoyable.

- Helps develop cognitive and tactical games awareness.

- Can be progressively overloaded by increasing the pace of the practice and limiting the time performers have to make decisions.

WALK-THROUGHS, RUN-THROUGHS AND REHEARSALS

Run-throughs or rehearsals of play is a useful development approach in many team games or choreographed activities. It allows players to become familiar with their roles and movements within the play before a competitive scenario. Walk-throughs and run-throughs can be gradually upped in intensity by increasing the pressure to be more game-like or competitive. At first walk-throughs could be unopposed or without music, then opposed passively or with music, until finally being opposed actively or without stopping the music.

Benefits of walk-throughs, run-throughs and rehearsals

- Individual areas of responsibility are practiced within set actions.

- Practices can be progressed from unopposed to actively opposed.

- Rehearsing an action help make the action automatic.

- Relieves anxiety, relaxes and calms nerves.

- Familiarises the mind with the desired outcome.

- Prepares groups and teams for competitive scenarios.

- Can help maintain motivation and preparation as the rehearsal can be done when performers not able to physically practice.

PASSIVE AND ACTIVE DEFENDER

As a development approach the use of passive and active defenders involves gradually building up the level of demand placed upon performers. These types of practices involve opponents who apply varying degrees of pressure. When defenders are passive, they are on the playing area to provide a visual physical barrier and little or no pressure is applied. This is useful when new tactics have been learnt as it provides the opportunity to see the strategy in a games context, without the pressure of active opposition.

During this type of practice you would gradually build up to using more active defenders, who can move, react and eventually fully challenge and oppose your attack. This allows performers to experience small amounts of pressure at a time and build up to the full pressure they would experience in a competitive game. This additional time and space will allow them to practice without anxiety and helps develop their decision-making and problem-solving skills in a more game-like situation.

Benefits of passive and active training

- Limited pressure makes it easier to concentrate on performing the identified technique or tactic.
- Can be adapted to suit individuals performance needs.
- Can be performed in a conditioned game-like situation.
- Develops awareness of performing with defenders in appropriate positions.
- Tactics can be practiced in realistic game-like situations.
- Encourages performers to adapt and learn to cope with the demands of performing identified skills or tactics under pressure.
- Can be progressively overloaded as you gradually build up the pressure of defenders.

The table shows examples of progression from passive to active defence in basketball and rugby.

ACTIVITY	PASSIVE		ACTIVE
Basketball	Defender still, hands behind back	Hands behind back, one step allowed	Full movement using arms and hands
Rugby	Defender stands still	Defender moves to ball but can not tackle	Defender has full movement and can tackle

 THINGS TO DO AND THINK ABOUT

1. Describe a modified or adapted strategy you have taken part in.
   (a) Explain in detail what you did, where you did it, when you did it and how you prepared the session.
   (b) Explain the benefits of this type of training in relation to your chosen activity and the type of fitness required for you to perform successfully.
   (c) State why you used this method of training, referring to your chosen activity.

2. Repeat Q1 describing a walk-through, rehearsal and practices where the defender was passive/active that you have taken part in.

3. Consider and list the limitations of each training method.

 DON'T FORGET

When learning it is important to practice more passively, in order to experience success. As you approach the autonomous stage of learning you need to practice under increased pressure, with more active defenders, as this replicates the performance situation more.

ONLINE TEST

Complete the test at www.brightredbooks.net on modifying and adapting strategies and walk-throughs and rehearsals and on passive and active defenders.

MEETING MENTAL PERFORMANCE DEVELOPMENT GOALS

Many experts and athletes believe that successful performance is 90% in the mind. They believe that in training the mind to be still, focussed and controlled, performance will be enhanced. When performers worry and think they will make a mistake they usually do, however when they positively focus on what they are going to do successfully to win then this is more likely to happen. Mental preparation is vitally important to performer's success.

MENTAL IMAGERY AND VISUALISATION

Mental imagery or visualisation involves a performer imagining themselves in an environment and performing a specific activity successfully. It involves using all of their senses – sight, hearing, feel and smell. The images should show the performer with finesse and feeling happy with their performance. This development approach is based on the theory that your mind does not distinguish between reality and imagination, so if you can visualise yourself being successful then there is no reason why your mind cannot manifest this occurring.

The use of imagery primes athletes muscles to perform the correct skills or technique and to successfully execute the appropriate actions during competition and it conditions their mind to think clearly and calmly about how they will react to certain pressures, situations and problems. Elite athletes consider it to be their mental warm-up.

Benefits of mental imagery and visualisation

- Complex skills, sequences or tactics can be perfected.
- The performer becomes familiar with the competition tactics, routines, set plays or course layout.
- Effective mental warm-up and preparation.
- Helps to relieve muscular tension and anxiety whilst promoting mental arousal.
- Establishes a positive mental state which increases confidence.
- Reduces negative thoughts by focusing on positive outcomes.
- Allows a performer to see themselves performing successfully.
- Focuses the mind before competition.

"I have sat on Centre Court with no one there and thought a bit about the court, the matches I have played there, [...] I want to make sure I feel as good as possible so I have a good tournament."

Andy Murray describing preparing mentally

"I never hit a shot even in practice without having a sharp in-focus picture of it in my head. It's like a colour movie. First, I 'see' the ball where I want it to finish, nice and white and sitting up high on the bright green grass. Then the scene quickly changes, and I 'see' the ball going there: its path, trajectory, and shape, even its behaviour on landing. Then there's a sort of fade-out, and the next scene shows me making the kind of swing that will turn the previous images into reality and only at the end of this short private Hollywood spectacular do I select a club and step up to the ball."

Jack Nicklaus, golfer

RELAXATION TECHNIQUES

Relaxation can be useful as a development approach for mental preparation in a number of circumstances. All relaxation techniques will help release tension in muscles by promoting concentration on control of breathing, and relieving unhelpful sensations. Some relaxation techniques will use mental imagery to achieve this. For this technique to work, it is essential that the performer believes that relaxation will help and must undertake relaxation in a quiet and warm room, free from interruptions.

Some examples of relaxation techniques are shown in the table.

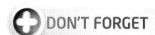
VIDEO LINK

Watch the clip at www.brightredbooks.net showing how to relax during sport.

RELAXATION TECHNIQUE	DESCRIPTION
Centring	Focus your attention on the centre of your body, focus on your breath and maintain your attention on your centre whilst thinking of a specific chosen word.
Meditation	Lie on your back or sit comfortably, relax your muscles and focus on your breath whilst breathing through your nose. Do not let your attention drift.
5 Breath	In a comfortable position of your own choosing, inhale slowly and deeply through your nose and exhale through your mouth, perform a body scan and continue.
Benson's relaxation response	Pick a focus word with meaning to you, relax and breathe repeating this word, be passive and dismiss any other thoughts that enter your mind.
Cognitive techniques – imagery	Imagine yourself in a calm and controlled situation, which can take the form of mental rehearsal, kinaesthetic imagery or creative imagery. This can be used to help relax and focus.
Thought stopping	Refusal to think negatively, instead substituting this with positive thought, can be used before or during competition or an event.
Positive self-talk	Confirm your own ability by repeating positive affirmations to yourself and eliminating the negative self chatter.
Rational thinking	Focus inwardly on the internal. Evaluate the situation and its logical consequences. This stops anxiety growing from the imbalance of perception on the situational demands.
Somatic techniques – biofeedback	Measure the physical changes that happen to the body when anxious. Measuring and training in this way can help you control the physiological effects of muscular tension to adopt a calmer state.
Progressive muscular relaxation	Increase the tension of the muscles and then relax each muscle group in turn.

Benefits of relaxation techniques

- Promotion of rest, recovery and recuperation.
- Easy to perform with practice.
- Removes stress-related reactions such as muscular tension or anxiety.
- Establishes a physical and mental state which is more receptive to positive mental imagery.
- Eliminates all negative thoughts and feelings.
- Can be altered to suit the demands of the performance situation.
- Arouses performers both physically and mentally prior to the warm-up.

DON'T FORGET

If 90% of performance is in your mind then you need to train your mind as you train your body, using any of the techniques mentioned. *'Whatever the mind can conceive and believe it can achieve.'* Napoleon Hill

THINGS TO DO AND THINK ABOUT

1 Describe how you used visualisation and relaxation techniques as development approaches.

   (a) Explain in detail what you did, where you did it, when you did it and how you prepared the session.

   (b) Explain the benefits of this type of training in relation to your chosen activity and the factor required for you to perform successfully.

   (c) State why you used this method of training, referring to your chosen activity.

2 Consider and list the limitations of each technique.

ONLINE TEST

Complete the test at www.brightredbooks.net on visualisation and relaxation techniques.

MEETING EMOTIONAL PERFORMANCE DEVELOPMENT GOALS

TEAM TALKS

Team talks are usually given by a coach or manager to the team or player prior or during a competition. It involves a rundown of the tactics alongside an opportunity to emotionally charge players and get them motivated for the competition. This process gets them mentally ready prior to the fixture and is an important development approach for emotional factors.

Team talks are extremely useful as they can change the attitude and mind-set of players at crucial stages of a game. The style of talk will alter based on knowledge of individuals and the different ways they need to be motivated. Some players react positively to receiving detailed instructions given in a quiet and controlled manner, whereas others react better to managers who show more emotion.

Benefits of team talks

- Gives an opportunity to recap the tactics and strategies to be used.
- Begins to mentally prepare performers for the task ahead.
- Emotionally charges performers and arouses them for competition.
- Unites players or groups before they need to work together as a team.
- Can be adapted to suit the demands of the performance situation.

VIDEO LINK

Watch the clip at www.brightredbooks.net showing a team talk prior to an American football game in a movie starring Al Pacino.

DON'T FORGET

The benefits and limitations for many of these approaches are transferable. Therefore your knowledge can be applied across a variety of approaches.

Recently, Jose Mourinho was reported as walking into the Chelsea changing room at half time when they were losing to tell the players to get themselves out of this mess and then walked out. Chelsea went on to win the game.

Alex Ferguson was known as a shouter and ruled the changing room through fear and an iron fist.

Arsene Wenger is a more methodical manager who is calm and will encourage his players to improve technical aspects without raising his voice and not showing too much obvious emotion.

ASSERTIVENESS TRAINING

Assertiveness training is designed to train performers to avoid being bullied, put down and out-muscled. Assertiveness is about having the confidence to resist those who seek to dominate and manipulate you. In sporting contexts, having this strength of character will ensure that you perform successfully in the face of opposition and meet your performance demands.

Three of the key assertive techniques are:

- broken record
- fogging
- negative assertion.

TECHNIQUE	EXPLANATION	EXAMPLE
Broken record	In the broken record technique, a request is repeated over and over again until the desired response is obtained or a workable compromise is reached. Attempts at distraction or changing the subject are resisted.	When performer makes up excuses to avoid training, a coach would use the broken record technique to continually remind the athlete of the benefits of training. They do not give up until they get the desired response.
Fogging	Fogging involves training yourself to stay calm in the face of criticism, and agreeing with whatever may be fair and useful in it. By refusing to be provoked and upset by criticism, you remove its destructive power.	When an opponent tries to wind you up with trash talk, you refuse to become upset and deny your critic the satisfaction of seeing you being intimidated. This will result in them eventually leaving you alone and empowered in your role.
Negative assertion	When someone who is criticising you has a valid point, this technique allows you to take responsibility for judging your own performance. Acknowledging all feedback allows you to have control and learn from these mistakes.	If you do not train to your full capacity, own up to it and show the coach that you plan on doing extra sessions to make up the deficit. Do not give up or think you can not make up for it.

Benefits of assertiveness training

- Can help the performer recognise when they are being manoeuvred for someone else's benefit.

- Desire to overcome the problem or task, and development of skills and habits to overcome that problem.

- Helps performers resist such treatment effectively without becoming angry and aggressive.

- Helps performers cope with criticism.

- Rehearses successful habits until they are perfect.

- Feeling of satisfaction and enjoyment in performing the skill.

- Repeated goal-setting in order to progress and maintain motivation.

 THINGS TO DO AND THINK ABOUT

1 Describe a time when you have experienced a team talk.
   (a) Explain in detail what you heard, what its purpose was, when it occurred and how it prepared you.
   (b) Explain the benefits of this type of training in relation to your chosen activity and the factor required for you to perform successfully.
   (c) State why you used this method of training, referring to your chosen activity

2 Repeat Q1 describing a time you used assertiveness training.

3 Consider and list the limitations of team talks and assertiveness training.

 DON'T FORGET

Training your emotions helps you maintain positive self-esteem and levels of arousal. Emotions can play a large part in performance, and learning to channel your emotional energy can be the key to success.

 **DON'T FORGET**

We can be the master of our own thoughts but we may also be a slave to our own emotions. If we have a balance of the two, what may we then achieve?

 ONLINE TEST

Complete the test at www.brightredbooks.net on team talks and assertive training.

MEETING SOCIAL DEVELOPMENT GOALS

Your role within a team, your interactions with team members, opponents and officials are all elements of social factors that can impact on you, and your team's success. There are a number of development approaches that work on the social factors that can help your performance. Within this section, we will look at team-building and restorative practice.

DON'T FORGET

There are also many more development approaches which you may already have used in your PE course.

TEAM BUILDING EXERCISES

VIDEO LINK

Watch the clip at www.brightredbooks.net to see some examples of team building activities.

Team building exercises involve different types of activities that are aimed at enhancing social relations and clarifying team members' roles. These activities frequently assign tasks for performers to solve through collaborative means. They are inclusive and promote performers self-esteem and ability to work together towards a shared goal. The table shows some examples of tasks used in team building exercises.

EXAMPLE	EXPLANATION
Human knot	Group stands in a circle. Each person holds another persons hand across the circle. Repeat with remaining hand. Then the group must work together to unravel the massive human knot.
Build a bridge	Split group into equal teams. Give each team a bowl of water and objects to build the bridge over the water. Set the time and once time is up, each group demonstrates how well their bridge works by adding weights to it one at a time.
Tug-of-war	Split team into two groups. Teams compete to pull opposing side over a line using rope.
Paintballing	In two teams players work together to defend their flag whilst attacking their opponents. Players have guns with paint in them to defend themselves and if shot the player is out.

Examples of team building exercises

contd

Benefits of team building exercises

- Includes all team members with clearly defined roles and responsibilities.
- Builds trust and respect.
- Improves ability to be creative and solve problems.
- Improves self-esteem and motivation.
- Promotes team work and collaboration.
- Allows players to socialise together and have fun outside their activity.
- Ensures that players get to know one another well.
- Improves morale and highlights leadership skills.
- Identifies teams strengths and weaknesses.

RESTORATIVE PRACTICES

Restorative practices are talking strategies that promote harmonious relationships in teams and can lead to the successful resolution of conflict. The aim of restorative practices is to develop a sense of community and to manage conflict and tensions by repairing and building relationships. These practices can be used to create an environment where common goals are agreed, discussed and achieved by team-mates or by coaches and athletes through building a sense of community and empowerment.

Restorative practices may also help in situations where team harmony or coach–performer relations have been damaged by the actions of one party. Restorative approaches require the individual to take responsibility for their actions and start a process which aims to repair damage done and solve any problems caused, so the group can move forward together.

Benefits of restorative practices

- Assists in the management of conflict and tension.
- Creates an environment where common goals are agreed.
- Enables a team to move forward together.
- Promotes the harmony of a team and importance of all members.
- Strengthens relationships between performers and the coaching team.
- Improves performance outcomes of the group.

KEEP
CALM
and USE
Restorative
Practices

 **DON'T FORGET**

You should be able to recognise some limitations to these approaches from your knowledge gained in earlier sections.

 THINGS TO DO AND THINK ABOUT

1 Describe a time when you have experienced team building exercises.
   (a) Explain in detail what you heard, what its purpose was, when it occurred and how it prepared you.
   (b) Explain the benefits of this type of training in relation to your chosen activity and the factor required for you to perform successfully.
   (c) State why you used this method of training, referring to your chosen activity.

2 Repeat Q1 describing a time you used restorative practice.

3 Consider and list the limitations of the development approaches you have used.

 ONLINE TEST

Complete the test at www.brightredbooks.net on team building and restorative practice.

RECORDING, MONITORING AND EVALUATING PERFORMANCE

WHY DO WE RECORD, MONITOR AND EVALUATE PERFORMANCE?

What's Next?

INTRODUCTION

Performance should be monitored and evaluated throughout development programmes and at different phases of a competitive season. This ensures you progress as planned and helps inform adaptations/interventions when necessary. This can include changes to intensity, frequency, duration and competitive elements of a programme.

A wide variety of tools can be used.

THE IMPORTANCE OF RECORDING, MONITORING AND EVALUATING PERFORMANCE

Recording, monitoring and evaluating are part of the same process, but have distinct purposes. It is vital that you understand the difference between them.

- **Recording** captures benchmark data. This provides a valuable contrast throughout a season. It is the setting down of something which can later be referenced and compared. You officially display a score or something measurable which you have achieved.
- **Monitoring** ensures progress is as planned and, if it isn't, helps with the design of suitable interventions. It involves systematic observations to check the progress or quality of training or sessions over a period of time.
- **Evaluating** measures success and analyses what aspects of training have worked (and not worked), what you have learnt about yourself as a result and why. It involves assessing the impact of recent changes and alteration in your performance, when you judge or appraise how successful your PDP has been.

When monitoring, information should be recorded using a variety of methods. This ensures that improvements are being made and can be used to inform future decisions about the adaptations that may be needed to your personal development plan (PDP).

DON'T FORGET

To answer an evaluate question you need to state how **useful** the method, approach, tool or programme was, how **appropriate** and how **effective** you believe the method, approach, tool or programme was.

WHY MONITOR AND EVALUATE?

The main purpose is to ensure the appropriate interventions are made if performance goals or expectations are not being met. Other reasons are:

- You can check whether your development plan is appropriate to your individual needs. Are you working on the right things?
- You can assess performance strengths/weaknesses, and decide if they are improving.
- You can compare pre- and post-training data to see if specific improvements have been made. For example, are you now able to score higher in a particular fitness test?
- Information received from monitoring helps you set new targets and goals. When you reach a certain level or achieve a target or goal, you should reassess and set new targets in order to keep challenging yourself to improve further.
- You can identify if training is at the correct intensity. If your training is too hard, you will be unable to complete it or if it is too easy, no improvement will be made.
- You can evaluate whether improvement has been made at the specific areas you targeted. Has your training actually worked. Can you now jump higher when you go to spike the ball?
- You can evaluate if your training has made a specific impact on your performance in a whole game situation. A training match may be included as part of your PDP.
- Monitoring your improvement informs decisions on progressing your training as required. How quickly have you progressed and how quickly can your training progress to keep challenging you?

DON'T FORGET

In this course you may be asked to **explain** the purpose of monitoring and evaluating.

DON'T FORGET

Monitoring and evaluating differ as monitoring occurs throughout the process while evaluating occurs at the end.

contd

- You can calculate if short-term and long-term goals have been achieved.

Monitoring

Monitoring is an **ongoing** process. It is something you will carry out **regularly** and **during** your development plan.

Evaluating

This is a process you will carry out at the **end** of your training. You will **sum** up what has happened and draw a conclusion **based upon** the **evidence.**

Methods used to monitor and/or evaluate

The methods you use to monitor can also be used to evaluate (**unless you are asked to give a different method**), however, the difference is that your answer **must** make reference to **when** you carried out the method.

USE OF PROTOCOLS FOR RECORDING

If any comparison is to be made between data gathered, it is vital that the conditions of analysis (protocol) are consistent and are exactly the same each time (or as close as is possible). If conditions of analysis are constant all of the methods of gathering information can be repeated and initial and final data can be compared with a high degree of validity and reliability.

The aspects that you need to consider when establishing protocols are:
- **Environmental considerations** – if your initial gathering took place indoors then future data should be gathered indoors.
- **Playing conditions** – did you gather data while playing a match? Make sure your comparison is not against a practice situation. Match conditions are less predictable and you would not get a reliable result.
- **Opposition** – your competitors will offer a different challenge and if they are not evenly matched to yourself, or the competitor you faced before, then the data you gather will be less reliable.
- **Who else was involved?** You must try to use the same observer, the same feeder, in order to keep the conditions as near as possible to each other.
- **Criteria for assessment** – are they exactly the same, is the observer in a similar mood or are they distracted?
- **Time of day**, **day of week** – if completed in the morning after a competitive performance then it needs to be done at exactly the same time the next time.

Evaluation of a development plan

To **evaluate** the effectiveness of your development plan and the methods used to monitor development you will need to:
- decide whether or not your development plan was successful
- provide evidence to justify how you drew conclusions (**evaluative statements** that will enable you to discuss)
- evaluate the effectiveness of your development plan.

Decide how useful and appropriate the methods you used to monitor your development were and justify your reasons. You should make reference to the following aspects in your response:

○ ease of use	○ accuracy	○ reliability	○ specificity
○ measurable	○ validity	○ repeatability	

By considering the points above, you will be able to make reference to the **advantages** and **limitations** that exist within any method used. This will help you structure your answers on the appropriateness so you can provide suitable justification for any method, approach or programme that you have chosen to use.

THINGS TO DO AND THINK ABOUT

1 What is meant by the terms recording, monitoring and evaluating?

2 Explain the purpose of monitoring and evaluating.

METHODS AND TOOLS FOR MONITORING, RECORDING AND EVALUATING

DON'T FORGET

Training diaries allow you the opportunity to verbalise your thoughts on training and how you feel you are progressing.

ONLINE

Visit www.brightredbooks.net to see an example of a training diary entry. Notice that this performer comments on both the physical and mental factors.

ONLINE

Head to www.brightredbooks.net to complete the quick quiz.

ONLINE

Visit www.brightredbooks.net and consider the performance situations outlined.

DON'T FORGET

If you are getting fitter your heart rate will decrease as the efficiency of your oxygen transport system improves. However if you are not benefiting from training then you may not see any decrease. If you failed to complete your programme and missed sessions then your heart rate may increase and give you away.

DON'T FORGET

HRMs measure the physical fitness sub-factor cardio-respiratory endurance. They cannot be used to measure other physical fitness factors.

METHODS AND TOOLS FOR MONITORING AND RECORDING

Training diary

Training diaries are very useful to record notes on your performance development. A training diary lets you gather **qualitative** data about how you feel the session went; how you feel you performed; how much you completed; whether you think it was set at the correct intensity; and the impact that you feel or see that training is having on your overall performance. **Quantitative** data can also be recorded such as scores, distances, times or reps managed to provide benchmarks to compare throughout your sessions. Your training diary should be specific to your development programme and is a useful and appropriate place to comment on all of the factors that appear in your PDP.

Heart rate monitors

Some heart rate monitors (HRMs) use a chest strap with sensors which transmit data to a watch on your wrist, which can display the data in real time. Others use optical sensors in wrist-worn devices such as watches or fitness trackers. Most will let you set suitable training zones so you can be alerted to your heart rate as you carry out a session, and give feedback through beeps or vibrations to change intensity if you move out of the desired training zone. Some items of gym equipment have HRMs built in, so by wearing the chest belt your heart rate will be displayed on the front panel. This can give important information about the intensity you are working at and ultimately are capable of. This gives useful measurable data about your **cardio-respiratory endurance**.

Retesting

Retesting lets you compare different sets of results and check for improvements. To be valid, it is important that the same protocols are used and all recording is undertaken in the same conditions. This ensures data is accurate and can reliably be used to measure progress.

Knowledge of results

After every performance you should record your result. If you perform every week, you will have a lot of results to compare and contrast by the end of a season or training programme. Having knowledge of the results of your competitions will provide measurable and reliably comparable data to analyse and interpret. This information can assist you to determine whether your training programme is progressing to plan or not. It can also give you social information about venues where you perform well or badly, providing further information that could assist your development planning.

Game statistics

Game statistics can be gathered after you perform using a variety of different technologies, or they could be completed using the information gathered from

contd

observation schedules. With observation schedules, an unbiased and knowledgeable observer watches you perform and charts information that you have agreed you wish to have prior to the performance. This could be scores, scorers, points total, points breakdown, splits, starting time, discipline records, corners won/conceded, and so on. The information you choose to have recorded should give you useful detail regarding the progress of your development programme and the factors that you are trying to improve.

Feedback

Feedback based on information or reactions on your performance of a task is a great monitoring tool. Feedback can be given in a variety of forms:
- **Verbal** – when a coach, teacher or peer provides an account of your performance and suggestions to assist you to develop
- **Written** – when you receive a detailed report of your stats, training outputs and new targets or goals or suggestions
- **Visual** – when technology is used to let you observe and reflect on your performance for yourself, allowing you to take ownership of giving feedback
- **Kinaesthetic** – when you feel for yourself how you have done and internally can process what needs to happen to correct or develop the action further
- **Auditory** – when a crowd or audience show appreciation for your performance then you become aware of your successes and progress, this raises your confidence

EVALUATING YOUR PERFORMANCE

In order to **evaluate** the success of your development plan you will draw on the information collected when you monitored your performance. This will enable you to decide upon your future development needs. Here are some examples:
- What aspect of fitness were you trying to improve? Explosive power, speed, strength agility etc.
- What method did you use to gather information on the chosen aspect that you would also use to monitor your progress? Standardised fitness test, match fitness analysis table, timed observation table etc.
- At what stages did you monitor using the method and why? Start/middle/end or start and end or after each week/session etc.
- How did this help you to evaluate your performance? What did the results tell you?
- How was your performance impacted? How were you now coping in a game situation?

From an understanding of all the above, you can work out your future development needs:
- Do you need to do anything to maintain or continue improving this aspect?
- Has the monitoring process highlighted any other weaknesses in your performance that need attention?
- How will working on your future development needs impact positively on your performance?

It is important to constantly evaluate the effectiveness of your PDP both during the duration of the programme and after it has been completed. You will already have **initial** data (pre-development plan) that has given you a starting point for your training. The information you gather during and after your plan will be compared to your baseline data. During the programme, you should be retesting after every session, after a couple of sessions or after a week of training. This enables you to assess and measure any improvement in performance and the level of effectiveness of training in order to offer suggestions for further improvement. This may lead to adaptations within your PDP.

 THINGS TO DO AND THINK ABOUT

When you are answering a question about evaluating your performance you should make it personal to you. Relate your answer to the differences in your performance. Use the information above to help you **evaluate** and remember this is one of the four **command** words.

 **DON'T FORGET**

Retesting provides you with valuable data to compare and contrast as you monitor and check for improvements.

 **DON'T FORGET**

Knowledge of results is a monitoring tool that provides you with information regarding how successfully you performed.

 **DON'T FORGET**

The statistics you gather on your games provide a useful insight into your competitive performance and the aspect of your performance that is most important to develop.

 ONLINE TEST

Head to www.brightredbooks.net to test your knowledge of monitoring and recording methods.

 ONLINE

Complete the table at www.brightredbooks.net to evaluate your performance.

PLANNING YOUR PERFORMANCE DEVELOPMENT PLAN (PDP)

INTRODUCTION

After you have gathered information on your performance the next step is to analyse that information in order to identify the current strengths and weaknesses of your performance. When you are aware of what these are you will know more clearly what in particular you would like to develop in order to improve your overall performance. When planning your performance development you need to consider a number of different things. These include:

- your level of fitness, stage of learning or previous experience
- the phase of the season, or time left until competition
- the activity and role within that activity that you are training for
- your individual strengths and weaknesses
- the strengths and weaknesses of your whole team, tactical considerations
- principles of training, effective practice, and play
- environmental considerations, such as the surface that you will play on
- methods of monitoring, recording and measuring your success.

By considering all these elements, you will ensure that the programme you create is specific for your individual and team needs. This will ensure that it is appropriate to your level of ability and that you will give yourself the best chance of steadily improving. It will prevent you being de-motivated, which can happen if sessions are too easy or hard, and will ensure your performance does not plateau or fail to improve.

Most people will seek help from coaches and teachers when formulating a development plan. Alternatively, you may be given a generic plan and told to adapt it to suit your own needs. Generally, like most things, the more preparation and thought that goes into the planning stage the more likely that it is going to be successful and appropriate. If you don't prepare adequately, you may find you need to make more changes during or after sessions. A thorough approach to monitoring will help identify when the programme is not suited to you, enabling you to act to rectify the situation and make adaptations where necessary.

INITIAL OR BASELINE DATA

Initial, or baseline, data recorded at the start of a programme, is vital in providing a benchmark for the duration of a development programme and season. Examples of baseline data could be standardised tests, observation schedules, profiling wheels, scatter diagrams or a questionnaire. Some of these methods could allow you to compare your results against the standard norms tables or model performers so that you can measure yourself next to other performers. Baseline data provides a permanent record and point of reference which is used for comparison when you decide to retest or monitor your PDP.

When making comparisons you will consider the following:
- What has improved?
- Has anything weakened?
- How much by? (Can you quantify? This will not always be possible.)
- What impact are these differences having on my overall performance?

Remember that you can draw on all four factors here. Most aspects that you develop will have a knock-on effect to something else. For example, you might be working on the social factor and aim to develop group dynamics but if you are effective here you will also realise that your mental and emotional factors are affected here as your confidence and motivation are also likely to improve.

Once the comparisons have been made you need to decide what impact the results will have on your development, how they affect your PDP and how you ensure that you continue to improve.

DON'T FORGET

Development planning needs to be specific to performers individual needs. Consideration must be taken of fitness, stage of learning, experience, the role within activity and the environmental and tactical constraints placed on the performer.

DON'T FORGET

Planning is time-consuming but if done correctly it will benefit you in the long run.

DON'T FORGET

Gathering initial or baseline data is key to your performance development plan. This information provides data to be compared and contrasted throughout training.

ONLINE

Visit www.brightredbooks.net to see an example of how you may record your initial, during and post development data.

ONLINE

Visit www.brightredbooks.net to see some model answers on evaluating performance and what it means for your future development needs.

EXAM CRAFT

INTRODUCTION

Your question paper is worth 40 marks. Split over two sections.

- Section 1 is worth 24 marks and is made up of three questions.
- Section 2 is worth 16 marks and is made up of one question with two parts. The allocation of marks can be an 8/8 split or a 10/6 split.

Your exam time is 90 minutes. Therefore you have 2.25 minutes per mark. This gives roughly 9 minutes for a 4 mark question. You should prepare to give yourself around 35 mins to complete your scenario. If you get stuck move on, don't sit around looking into space. Come back if you have time later.

DON'T FORGET

This includes reading and thinking time so you are probably writing for about 7 minutes per question.

BREAKING DOWN THE EXAM

There could be a maximum of 16 marks available for any one factor:

- 8 marks in section 1 and
- 12 marks in section 2

It is important to know that marks can be allocated differently in the scenario (section 2). See the example below:

Q4. Your answer must make reference to **emotional** factors and one other factor that you select from physical, mental or social.   (8)

You will then be given some data to apply your knowledge of the factors to.

Marks can be allocated on a 4/4 split:

- 4 marks for **emotional** factor and 4 marks for **other** factor **or**
- 6 marks for **emotional** factor and 2 for the **other** factor – **please note that this does not work the opposite way.** The 6 marks can only be awarded for the factor that is **stipulated** in the exam. In this case the **emotional** factor.

COMMAND WORDS

Describe, explain, analyse and **evaluate** are the four **command** words that you must fully understand in order to answer questions throughout the exam. There are four essential command words throughout this course. They appear within the unit assessment and form the basis for **course assessment** and in your factors impacting on performance booklet. These words will form questions that can relate to

- factors impacting on performance
- gathering information
- developing performance.

The command words mean:

- **Describe** – give a detailed account using words stating exactly what you did. Paint a picture of what you see, giving a detailed account of something.
- **Explain** – make a situation clear to someone by giving the relevant facts to provide reasons for an action.
- **Analyse** – explain something methodically that you have discovered or revealed through closely examining details.
- **Evaluate** – give a judgment to value or assess the impact of recent changes in performance and its success.

How to answer a 'describe' question

Who ▶ What ▶ Where ▶ When ▶ How

The command word **describe** is asking you to give a detailed account of something. To answer a describe question you must leave no detail to chance and systematically state exactly **what** you did, **how** you did it, **where** this occurred, **who** exactly was involved and **when** exactly you did it. You are trying to paint a picture in words (sometimes by drawing) of something. Think about providing the characteristics or features of it.

EXAM CRAFT (CONTD.)

DON'T FORGET

To answer an explain question state **what** you did, **why** you did it, **justify** your decisions, state **how** they were **appropriate** and state the **impact**.

ONLINE

Head to www.brightredbooks.net to see two examples of how a candidate may answer a question asking them to explain how they monitored their development programme.

DON'T FORGET

You should access past paper questions from previous exams to give you practice at answering these types of questions. It is vital that you consider the following before attempting to write anything.

How to answer an 'explain' question

The command word **explain** is asking you to make something clear to another person by describing the relevant facts that provide the reasons and justification of an action or event. To satisfy an explain question you need to say **what you did** and back it up by stating **why you did it**, whilst justifying **why** you made **certain decisions, how they were appropriate** and state the **impact that they had**.

Your answer could include some of these words or statements:
- Because...
- This allowed me to...
- so that...
- This means that...

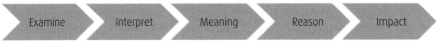

What ▸ Why ▸ Justify ▸ How ▸ Appropriateness ▸ Impact

How to answer an 'analyse' question

The command word **analyse** is asking you to identify the important parts of your method and approach and make the connections between them. To answer this question you need to scrutinise your data methodically and examine it carefully. Through that process you recognise and understand certain information that can justify whether or not your development programme has been successful.

When analysing you are expected to **examine** the data and interpret it to provide **meaning** and **reason**. To do this, you must state more information than is asked for in the question, and judge what you think this means, you must **justify** your **reasoning** and then state what the **impact** is for your performance.

Examine ▸ Interpret ▸ Meaning ▸ Reason ▸ Impact

The answer should use some of the following lead-in statements:
- This method/approach shows me that...
- This then allows for...
- As a result of this I can...
- This resulted in me...
- This approach/method/monitoring tool was appropriate because...

An example is:

> When examining the data I gathered on my social profiling wheel I found that I had scored high on inclusion and leadership. However I had dips in the wheel at the spike noted co-operation. This tells me that I feel less confident about my ability to co-operate and compete in a team than I do when I am in charge or leading. As a result of this I am going to monitor my co-operation closely in games and training and adopt some approaches to develop my co-operation. Hopefully the impact will be positive on my overall game performance.
>
> Mentally I gathered information on my performance using a Sports Competition Anxiety Test (SCAT). When I analysed this data I found that my anxiety began to set in prior to the competition and before I had even warmed up. I know this because of the questions I scored poorly in regarding how I felt in the lead up to the performance. I know from the questions I scored lowly on that I also failed to prepare myself physically and mentally by eating and resting enough before I competed. This information allows me to plan to focus on the pre-game period when planning to develop this weakness. This resulted in my overall game improving as I am less anxious before I begin. Hopefully meaning that I make less errors and mistakes at the beginning of the game.

'Evaluate' questions

Evaluate is one of the four **command** words you need to understand for this course. It asks you to **measure** how successful the method or approach was and **judge** how useful, appropriate and effective the method or approach is.

Some lead-in statements that could help you answer this type of question could include:
- 'The benefits of this method/approach were …'
- 'Improvements were clear when compared to ….'
- 'Results were above/below average/good/excellent' – provide numbers e.g. '50% effective'
- 'More useful than…' compared to another method
- 'This worked/did not work…'

ONLINE

Head to www.brightredbooks.net to see example questions and answers on monitoring and evaluating.

THINGS TO DO AND THINK ABOUT

1   Look at the three attempts a candidate made to describe how they gathered information on their performance.

> I did an analysis sheet during badminton. Basically I put ticks and crosses in the appropriate box after I had played a game. This gave me information on my performance so that I could improve.
>
> I used a match skills analysis in badminton. The table had 4 columns headed skills and quality features, effective shot, ineffective shot and % effective. All the skills were listed down the left hand side e.g. overhead clear, high service, smash etc. Across the top was the game that the skill occurred in. This was completed by an unbiased observer when I was playing a game of badminton against a player in my class of similar ability to myself. The observer understood the criteria I was being assessed against and used sound judgement to give ticks, crosses or question marks in the appropriate place.
>
> I used an observation schedule. This is a white sheet of paper that was marked with pen. Firstly I collected this sheet off of my teacher and then I collected my equipment so that I was ready to play after I put up the net and stands. I then did this with a partner so that it was quicker. Before we played we did a full warm-up to make sure we were prepared to participate fully. We then played and recorded our results before packing up again and handing my observation schedule into my teacher.

Use the 'who, what, where, when and how' method above to assess them. State what example is best and explain why.

2   Look through some sample questions, either online or that your teacher may have provided. In each question identify the **command word** (describe, explain, analyse, evaluate).

3   Identify exactly what is being asked. You could be asked about a process, a method, an approach, any impact, yourself, a model performer, or a combination of these things. Make sure you are clear about what is being asked and where in your folder you can access that information.

4   Be clear when the question has asked for information from – before, during or after development, monitoring, gathering or evaluating? Ensure you understand when and then check that this is correct by examining the questions around it.

5   Ensure you understand what factor(s) you are being asked about. Make sure it is the same factor and sub-factor that you have been focussing on throughout, or another if the question has specifically asked for this example.

6   'Think like a marker' – how much is the question worth and therefore how much detail is needed? Are there two parts to the question etc? Do you have similar quality, volume or tone of work as the sample answers you have read? If not what can you do to improve this.